THE TEEN'S GUIDE TO SAVING THE WORLD

THE TEEN'S GUIDE TO SAVING THE WORLD

AADITYA SENGUPTA DHAR

"Who's gonna save the world tonight?
Who's gonna bring it back to life?
We're gonna make it, you and I
We're gonna save the world tonight."

Save the World by Swedish House Mafia

"Words will be just words,
'Till you bring them to life"

Another World by One Direction

Anecdote Publishing House
E-35-A, E Block, Gali No. 2 Ganesh Nagar,
Pandav Nagar Complex Delhi-110092

Published by Anecdote Publishing House
Copyright © Aaditya Sengupta Dhar

First Edition 2023

ISBN 978-81-958907-9-8

MRP ₹ 350

All Rights Reserved.
No part of this publication may be reproduced, stored in a retrieval system, or transmitted in any form, or by any means—electronic, mechanical, photocopying, recording or otherwise—without the prior permission of the publisher. Opinions expressed in it are the author's own. The publisher is in no way responsible for these.
Book Promoted and Marketed by Champ Readers Pvt. Ltd.

Cover Design by Puja Sengupta
Layout by Graphic Tailor
Images Credit by Freepik.com
Printed by Nutech Print Services - India

CONTENTS

Foreword	ix
Introduction: No Superpowers, No Problem	1
Poverty Pulverizers	9
Hunger Games Heroes	23
Wellbeing Warriors	35
Education Electrifiers	47
Gender Equality Galvanizers	59
Water Warriors	71
Energy Exemplars	81
Growth Generators	91
Innovation Icons	101
Equality Enthusiasts	111
Sustainability Superstars	121

Role Models Of Responsibility   133
Climate Changemakers   145
Underwater Uplifters   155
The Land's Legends   163
Jumpstarting Justice   179
Partnering To Create A League Of Heroes   189

Bibliography   *195*
About The Author   *207*

FOREWORD

The Sustainable Development Goals (SDGs) were adopted by all United Nations Member States in 2015 to end poverty, reduce inequality and build more peaceful, prosperous societies by 2030. Also known as the Global Goals, the SDGs are a call to action to create a world where no one is left behind.

Making progress on these goals is key to resolving many of the challenges we face as a world- from sustainable cities to gender equality, to providing economic growth and well-being.

The SDGs cannot be achieved without the realization of child rights. As world leaders work to deliver on the 2030 promise, children around the globe are standing up to secure their right to good health, quality education, a clean planet, and more.

It is laudable that the young author of this work, Aaditya Sengupta Dhar, has, at a very early age, realised the significance of these, and also of how the younger generation can take the lead in being catalysts to the realization of these goals. His work brings to life many inspiring tales of teens who had stood up to make a difference in their communities in advancing these goals and should serve as an inspiration for other teens to realize their power in making a difference. Aaditya rightly says that teens should step up and take the lead in solving some of these issues so that they can have a more active voice in shaping the world they will inherit as adults.

He writes of many of the examples he cites as heroes and role models for teens around the world, and by taking the initiative to come up with this idea, write this book, and seek to engage and inspire fellow teenagers, Aaditya himself, perhaps without realizing it, emerges as a great role model for how he uses his passion for writing to strive to make a positive difference.

—**Rahul Bansal**
Head of Private Sector Partnerships & Fundraising,
UNICEF India

THE TEEN'S GUIDE TO SAVING THE WORLD

Rick Riordan

"Being a hero doesn't mean you're invincible. It just means that you're brave enough to stand up and do what's needed."

Chapter 1

INTRODUCTION
NO SUPERPOWERS, NO PROBLEM

Saving the world. Where have we seen that before? Infinity War, Endgame, Thor: Ragnarok. We saw a Norse Thunder god with a mighty hammer, multi-verse travelling sorcerers warping space and time, and a tech-genius billionaire forging impregnable superhuman suits.

What were they saving the world from? Aliens and psychopaths who would destroy our world to make theirs, with grand visions of ruling the Earth or moulding it to fit their philosophies.

Thank goodness Thanos isn't real. Thank goodness the world isn't locked in an eternal saga of villains and heroes blasting each other with flames, lasers and illusions. Thank goodness our world doesn't face such peril.

But we are in a world that does need saving. Its narrative may not feel as thrilling or grand as a Marvel blockbuster. There are no heroes gifted with godly powers or clear supervillains to fight.

That's the problem. The lack of such spectacular and imminent threats often blinds us to the real issues we face.

Our planet needs saving more than it ever has. The threats are everywhere: the Sixth wave of Animal Extinction, the catastrophes of the Climate Crisis, the darkness of poverty, and the turmoil faced by the victims of our unjust distribution of power, wealth, and opportunities.

The fate of billions hangs by a very thin string, a fragile strand that the winds of change threaten to snap.

If you are reading this book, you are probably like me, from a fairly privileged background, much more sheltered from the tumults of the world than most. However, imagine what the kids in the slum nearest to your house must be facing. Imagine what those farmers feel whose livelihood is threatened by climate change.

But why am I writing about this? I'm a teenager, about to turn fifteen in a few months. So, what investment do I feel I have in sweeping global problems?

Well, they may seem distant but they are pervasive and dangerous. They are often quite close to home if we keep our eyes open enough to see them.

From a young age, other species of animals fascinated me- exotic beings built so differently from humanity, from monkeys swinging through branches to slumbering koalas and Brobdingnagian hippos. Soon, though, I realised that these wonderful creatures were somehow "inferior" to us. That's what society wanted me to believe. When I was four, I learned that I was eating them. The chickens clucking in the farms, the fish from the sea- all were going into my stomach. Immediately, I turned vegetarian.

Come 2020. I am 12 years old. At my home, seated comfortably on a sofa, I see images on my television and phone screen that aroused something in me with their stark portrayal of realities so far removed from my own. Clips of endless lines of people- men, women, children cradled in their mother's arms- trudging on forlornly, harried by the sun, and the fatigue of walking for days in an age when airliners connect the whole world. They were trudging their way back to their villages, their livelihoods and lives ruined by COVID-19 and the resultant lockdowns in our cities.

I'd been enveloped in my cocoon, sheltered from the hardships of the outside world, which so many like me were bearing the brunt of. Now, the webbing that held it together, shielding me from the light outside, had been hewn apart, and a doorway stood open for me.

There was no looking back. I had to do something, something that went beyond philosophising and introspection and big words- something that made a difference and gave some relief to someone, somewhere.

Since the age of 9 or so, I had loved reading, in awe of the elaborate worlds created by fantasy authors such as JRR Tolkien (*The Lord of the Rings*) and Christopher Paolini (the *Inheritance Cycle*). My father is also a writer, and my parents read extensively. The walls of my home are lined with shelves full of books, from the cosy interior of the study to my bedroom.

Inspired by the books I'd read and by my father's journey, I started writing.

My first novel was a fantasy book titled *Secret Tails*, about an imaginary island country of advanced, intelligent animals who have influenced several moments in human history.

But what good is it to make and travel to new worlds that mimic ancient or medieval times, while our planet of the 21st century descends into chaos and catastrophe?

What good is it to use my passion and imagination to create new worlds, when the one I live in is threatened by myriad issues?

In 2020, after seeing those lines of migrant labourers trudging back to their villages, and inspired by the stories I'd read of famous people who came from humble backgrounds, I wrote *Underdogs,* which showcased the stories of icons like Milkha Singh, Narayan Murthy and others, who rose from humble beginnings to become legends. They had talent, they had grit, they had passion- but they all had something else- someone who believed in them, someone who gave them a chance. I wondered if one of the kids walking back to her village could have been the next PT Usha if only someone gave her a shot. I used this book to raise awareness of the fact that underprivileged children deserve a chance to unleash their potential, working in partnership with Save The Children India, and one of the high points of my life till then was when I was able to donate all earnings from book sales to Save The Children. It was a small step, but it kindled in me the belief that we can all make a difference.

Then, in 2021, I was part of the Take the World

Forward Fellowship, a program by Learn with Leaders in which we were taught about making an impact as teens. We could pitch an idea for a social initiative, and I suggested something close to my heart, which I felt could make a difference: a book called *Back from the Brink,* raising awareness of the problem of animal extinction in urban areas and what we could do to help out.

I set to work, conducting extensive primary and secondary research- surveys, books, and research papers. The secondary research told me that our cities are hotspots for endangered animals, home to half of the endangered species. This was an intriguing deviation from the stereotypes of endangered animals dwelling in nature reserves or the wild.

The primary research, however, was even more interesting.

What emerged was a desire and drive among people to contribute and support the cause- around 70% of respondents expressed a willingness to do so. But nearly none of them knew how they could do this, 88% saying they could only think of donating to NGOs. Further research revealed much everyone could do, with simple everyday steps such as helping stray cats and turning off the lights at night making a difference.

This taught me that most teens want to do something for the turbulent world around them. Indeed, there are several things they can do as young members of the community, but few are equipped with the knowledge and guidance they need for this.

That is where this book comes in. We do not need superpowers to save the world, just concern about what's happening, awareness, and translating that into purposeful action.

Saving the world in a Marvel movie is rather straightforward if challenging- defeating a villain or two, the sole threat to the stability of the planet.

In the real world, though, it is very evident that we are beset by an army of villains who threaten the foundations of our existence. The list goes on and on, myriad issues branching off into others.

Luckily, though, others have looked at this mess and tried to distil clarity from it.

The United Nation's seventeen Sustainable Development Goals (SDGs) are a good blueprint of what's needed to save the world. Too often, we see these as goals governments are responsible for fulfilling, and only speak about them during school assignments or academic discussions and debates. But distancing ourselves from them is not going to help.

The reality is that each of us can make a difference to these SDGs. As you'll see in this book, many teens are stepping forward to make a difference in their own way.

What am I trying to achieve through this book?

First, I hope you learn that while the world certainly looks messed up, it can be saved. Not by caped crusaders or celluloid superheroes, but by us.

I hope you are inspired by the stories I share of ordinary teenagers who are doing extraordinary things to make our world better. These are my heroes, and they should be yours. Kids like me and you, who didn't stop at bemoaning the state of the world but stood up to be counted; stood up to make a difference. These are the heroes we need, not caped crusaders, and these are the heroes you and I can aspire to emulate.

I hope you realize that there are simple, practical things we as teenagers can do every day to make a difference- to make the SDGs come to life and walk in the footsteps of some of these teenage heroes.

Who am I to tell you all this?

I'm not an eminent expert or grey-haired academic who has all the answers, just a teenager like you who has many questions about the world we live in. A teenager who feels the world needs fixing, and who better to fix it than us? After all, this is the world we will inherit as adults.

I've had many inspirations: My parents, who've instilled in me my values and the importance of trying to make a difference; my teachers at Ecole Mondiale World School who've encouraged me; Mr. Rahul Bansal of UNICEF for his mentorship; and finally, the teen heroes about whom I learned while writing this book.

The stories of the teens in this book, and the ideas and inspiration they spark should tell us that we can all make a difference.

We can all help make things a little bit better.

We can all help save our world.

We can all be heroes.

Nelson Mandela

"Overcoming poverty is not a gesture of charity. It is an act of justice."

Chapter 2

POVERTY PULVERIZERS

Imagine living in a slum. Imagine looking at the horizon and seeing cramped houses and waste-filled streets, choking at the stench of rotting waste and excreta, vision blurring and head spinning as you are overcome by dehydration and starvation.

Imagine your mother lying on the stone floor inside, coughing and sputtering as she struggles with Bronchitis.

These slums are everywhere in a city like Mumbai. We pass by them without even giving them a second thought or glance.

I passed by them every day, in my car or on the school bus. I had become accustomed to sights of ramshackle shacks and huts, the narrow alleys in between clogged with the reeking waste of plastic, thatch, and excreta.

I would see children playing in ragged, torn clothes or selling balloons to passers-by for money, or playing on the roadside when they should have been in school.

The sight of them, even up-close, unfortunately, does very little to move us and make us feel concerned about the issue. When was the last time you truly looked carefully at a scene in a slum?

When was the last time you did more than just process the smiles and torn clothing of the underweight children?

When was the last time you wondered what life must really be like, behind the smile, for the scrawny, underweight children in tattered clothes playing tag?

I am not preaching to you. I was the same. I would drive by these slums every day, in my comfortable cocoon. I was jolted out of that complacency and apathy in a way that changed my life.

***

COVID-19. 646 million infected. 6.6 million deaths.

Those are just statistics. Closer to home, we all know people who fell sick. I had COVID, and so did most of my friends. Our lives changed in many ways over those harrowing months- no in-person school, no going out, and no meeting friends.

However, I learned that others had it much, much worse.

What about the impact on 163 million lower-middle-class people in India, barely afloat in the pre-pandemic economy? They plunged beneath the surface, sucked into the whirlpool of poverty. The World Bank estimates that three to four years' worth of progress in fighting poverty has been lost due to the economic impact of the pandemic.

India is home to 40 million migrant workers, who came to cities from rural areas in the countryside in search of opportunities. They are generally used for low-skilled labour- construction, casual labour, and domestic help. These jobs are not well-paying but are essential, and thus provide stable employment.

Until all of them become obsolete in the wake of the sudden disappearance of many of the activities that make normal society what it is. Until millions of them are fired, forced out on leave, and have pay cuts. Until millions of them are left stranded without employment, savings, shelter, and food.

Until 11 million of them, with their families, are sent out on long, arduous treks for days, back to where they had come from.

That's what happened in the early days of the COVID lockdowns in India.

I saw the visuals on the TV news and my tablet as I scrolled to see what was happening in the world outside.

I saw in them more than physical exertion and evidence of financial turmoil- I took them as symbols, symbols of the pitiable status of India's poor. Come a crisis that grips the nation, and they are left out in the open, without any semblance of support and refuge.

Now, all of those memories of the harrowing scenes I had witnessed over the years came back to me in a deluge, breaking upon my mind with a new force. For a change, I saw those images as what they were, troubling snapshots from troubled lives, so different from our own that we can barely begin to imagine them.

I remembered stories I had read or heard of- Abdul Kalam and Milkha Singh's legendary rise from poverty to greatness and acclaim. This got me thinking- those children I'd seen in the slums might have been much more than met the eye.

One may be blessed with a naturally strong intellect, another with athleticism or strength. Beyond the surface, behind the realities of their difficult lives may be goldmines of potential and talent.

Perhaps, with the right opportunities- education, and support- this potential could be nurtured and unleashed, and some of those children could rise from the dirt that they came from and achieve greatness for themselves and their families.

That malnourished child in tattered clothing on the street, sharing $10m^2$ with five people, could be the next Abdul Kalam!

But who's going to make him that? Who is going to make him believe that such a thing, such a dream, is indeed possible?

I was now distressed, and restless. I had to do something. If I wouldn't, I would feel unfulfilled and incompetent, incompetent at making even the smallest of differences to something I felt strongly about.

I knew I couldn't just bring education and better housing and sanitation for a hundred families with the snap of my fingers, or, hell, even with a year's hard work. I was just a 12-year-old kid. So I decided to do something I knew I could.

I loved learning and I loved writing, and my parents had taught me that the best way to make a difference was to apply what you were good at and what you loved doing to solve problems others faced.

I began by researching. I researched extensively, looking through the lives of famous people I had known and admired for their achievements but rarely recognised for the hardships they had faced- from leaders like Abdul Kalam to business tycoons like Dhirubhai Ambani and Narayana Murthy to sportsmen such as Milkha Singh and Mary Kom.

I shortlisted twelve such people and outlined their stories in my mind. Then I started writing.

I included each of their tales, setting the stage of their humble beginnings and their childhood before putting forth the narrative of their quest to rise higher, with their initial efforts, usually followed by someone- a coach, a mentor, a parent, a friend- appreciating their capabilities and paving the path for them with the opportunities they needed.

They were all underdogs. They were all legends with humble beginnings, so that is what I made the title of my book- *Underdogs: Legends with Humble Beginnings*.

This experience taught me just how common such people are- who look beyond their surroundings and the environment they were born in. While I was writing this book, I saw an illustration of this while watching an India vs Australia cricket series. I learned that a debutant named

Thangarasu Natarajan had, till he was 28, played cricket with a tennis ball in the streets of Chinampatti.

I caught onto this as valuable material for my book, and his meteoric rise to the highest level of sport fascinated me.

I also found it striking that none of these icons did what they did alone. None of them was born so gifted and strong-willed and perfect that they were naturally built for greatness. Every single one of them needed someone who consistently and unfailingly stood by their side through their highs and lows. Abdul Kalam had his father. AR Rahman had his mother. Mary Kom had her coach. Milkha Singh was orphaned during the Partition, but he had support from his brother, who got him into the army, where an instructor kindled his passion for running.

We cannot count on all underprivileged children having the right combination of potential and luck to give them the ability, prosperity, and durability they require to achieve the extraordinary.

But if other members of society are compassionate and consistent in supporting these children, they stand a far better chance.

Here is where, I learned, organisations such as Save the Children India came in.

Much like the issue itself, my knowledge of NGOs fighting poverty had been just that- a vague conception in my mind of organisations taking donations from people and using those to help the poor. Had you asked me in Grade 6 to name one such NGO, you wouldn't have received any response worth speaking of.

Save the Children India is one of the most notable such NGOs, over 100 years old. Its initiative Bal Raksha Bharat has impacted 10 million children since 2008 alone, through education, protection from harm, health and nutrition projects, disaster relief work, etc.

I was not satisfied with just words on a page and changing the minds of a few readers about underprivileged children. I wanted to have a more concrete, direct impact.

I got in touch with the CEO of Save the Children India, Mr. Sudarshan Suchi. I spoke to him about my project and discussed Save the Children's work. He agreed to write the foreword to my book, and with his guidance and help, I was able to get the word out about my effort to many hundreds of thousands of people through Save the Children India.

The book was released on 23 January 2021. Within a few months, I donated all the money from the sales proceeds of the book to Save the Children India.

It was encouraging to know that my realisation and hard work were somewhat making up for twelve years of being oblivious to the challenges faced by those less privileged than I was.

As I lay in bed at night in June 2021 when I had made that first donation of my earnings, and looked pensively at the open sky outside, I exhaled deeply. Somewhere out there, a few children were sleeping better- perhaps with a fuller stomach, or a restful mind keen for the relaxation of sleep after spending a day learning at school. That thought comforted me and put me to sleep.

TEEN HEROES WHO ARE SAVING THE WORLD

That was just my story. A story close to me, the example of a teenager helping those in need in a way I know best. But there have been many other teenagers- and very young children, too- who were conscious about those suffering around them and have done greater things in the quest to fight poverty.

Peru struggles with the same menace as India and many other countries. In 2020, one in every three Peruvians lived in poverty.

There is a six-mile long, 10-foot barrier – the "Wall of Shame"- that divides the capital, Lima, into two- the "rich" and "poor" halves of the city. This is infamous for how blatantly it shows the world the economic disparity of the city.

One young boy, José Quisocala, born into a well-off family, was seven when he asked himself a simple question: why were there so many children living in poverty?

"There were children living in the streets, and I did not understand what was happening", he said in a 2022 interview.

"I just grasped that problem as if it were mine as if I was suffering from it; I wanted to make a difference."

When he looked at the children in Lima's *solares* (slums), he did not see nameless, obscure victims of misfortune. He saw kids like him with an existence very clearly different from his own, living in pathetically small, coloured shacks and huts in piles leading from the bases to the summits of the hills in the city.

These kids would spend their entire days scurrying across the streets, pulling wheelbarrows filled to the brim with *anticuchos* (marinated, spiced meat on a stick) or Peruvian barbecue with grilled beef, pork, and chicken mixed with potato.

There was a much darker side to what children did to earn a living, from mining to human trafficking. José likely knew about these too, and, given how deeply he empathised with the children, must have been shattered by such tidings.

"There were children working in the streets, and I did not understand what was happening".

When we think of helping to fight poverty, most of us intuitively think of giving the impoverished the facilities and opportunities that we have, and they lack- better education, for instance, or healthcare.

After all, these are the provisions that will allow people to lead healthier, more secure lives, and unleash their potential. Money is just a means to an end, a means to afford the necessities of life, right?

José thought slightly differently. A common saying goes, "Cure the cause, not just the symptoms".

Poverty is a condition measured not by access to services and the chance of survival, but by wealth- by USD and INR and Peruvian Sol. The root cause of all the ills associated with it is the deficiency of money.

José had been interested in finance for several years, so this came very naturally to him.

As he told The Guardian in his 2019 interview, "One

of the reasons why those kids were working was because there was no money at home. Why can't I teach them to save?"

He had also been concerned by environmental waste issues. His grandmother had taught him the importance of a clean environment, but he looked beyond the confines of his home and saw the mess outside, strewn about the streets. He determined one day in 2012 to combine his ecological concerns with his passion for finance and bringing children out of poverty.

He proceeded to become the youngest person on the planet to open his own bank.

The *Banco del Estudiante Bartselena* bank creates accounts for child clients filled with the funds generated from paying customers for the recyclable waste they pick. The children can then use this money at their discretion, such as for food or education.

2,500 children between 7 and 18 have used the bank to support their daily expenses. Demand for its services has skyrocketed, and it has risen from a small neighbourhood venture run by Jose, writing in his notebook, to a bank with 4,000 children being enrolled as we speak.

Two years after the bank's inception, Jose won UNICEF's International Prize. He won the Children's Climate Prize in 2018 for his role in reducing waste, and an accolade at the Young Activist's Summit in Geneva, in 2021.

His success and impact, and fulfilment in what he has achieved keep him going.

"What I do promotes equality, in equal opportunities for children, in quality of life, in access to education."

That, after all, is what ending poverty is all about.

YOUR GUIDE TO SAVING THE WORLD

Well, so what do we do for poverty? Do we establish banks? Do we write books?

There is much that can be done.

There are many charities and organisations that help fight poverty, in myriad ways.

For instance, Goonj is an organisation that sends a truck to a spot not far from my building every Sunday. It takes clothes and toys to be donated to the needy. Whenever my parents and I have spare items at home, especially on the eve of a big move when many are disposed of, we donate to Goonj.

There are several far larger bodies, such as Save the Children India, that impact millions of children through their initiatives in providing relief, education, healthcare, and much more. Encouraging your parents to donate to such NGOs gives them a great boost.

There are also several volunteer opportunities, such as the chance the organisation offers to become a Child Champion, have a voice and role in projects and get more opportunities to make a positive difference.

You could also do projects with your classmates and friends to have a positive impact on your neighbourhoods and communities. For instance, at my school in Grade 9, we did a project called ThriftShift in which we collected used clothes and modified them, before selling them at an auction. (More on this in the Responsible Production and Consumption chapter). This prevented the wastage of clothes, which would have contributed to climate change through decomposition in landfills.

Furthermore, the proceeds from the auction were donated to the SOS Children's Village in Alibaug, a home for underprivileged children who have lost their parents that gives them housing, education, a family, and opportunities to go higher in life.

I hope this has just whetted your appetite for more- since the next chapter is about hunger.

Anne Frank

"Hunger is not a problem, it's an obscenity. How wonderful it is that nobody need wait a single moment before starting to improve the world."

Chapter 3

HUNGER GAMES HEROES

When I was in the first grade, in 2015, the staff in the canteen praised me for never wasting my food. I was taken aback. I wasn't doing anything special, I was just eating, and not taking more than I needed. My parents sometimes joke that, back then, when I was still adjusting to living in a new country and a new school, that was one of the first pieces of positive feedback I got. To me, it wasn't a big deal, but as I grew, I learned that the food we take for granted can mean the difference between life and death to someone else.

I exit my school canteen during lunchtime each day at 1:40. Every time I exit, I am greeted with the sight of row upon row of trays in the racks, filled with half-finished meals of rice and dal and pasta. I see a boy pass before me, walking briskly on his way to play.

Casually, without even looking, he flicks his tray into the racks with a flourish and walks on. I look in it and see it littered all over with small handfuls of grains of rice strewn about, in pools of dal.

I see the staff come and rapidly scrape the leftover food off into a dustbin by the door.

At that very moment, a few hundred metres from our school, in the nearby slums, I know a child is going without lunch.

TEEN HEROES WHO ARE SAVING THE WORLD

As a species, we are doing very well in food production- in fact, too well. We eviscerate forests and maul undersea ecosystems with our massive nets, and desecrate fields, to supply our fast-multiplying population. Indeed, there is more than enough food produced on this planet to feed everyone.

Yet, the UN estimates that 924 million people are going hungry. Malnourished, undernourished, underfed.

High blood pressure, heart disease, and debilitation- the consequences of hunger are dire.

It causes 45% of child deaths worldwide.

Why do we live in a world where on the one hand, there is a problem of obesity and rampant Diabetes caused by over-indulgence, and on the other, the spectre of hunger and malnutrition?

As Anne Frank said, that is an obscenity. But we can help reverse it.

Florida. The land of glistening, pristine, sun-baked beaches, lush green swamps and wetlands stretching across millions of kilometres.

It is also the land of food insecurity, poverty, and starvation. The beautiful countryside is sprinkled with thousands of families who toil hard under the sun for the smallest servings on their tables. The sprawling cities are filled with homeless families lying, without shelter and livelihood, on the pavement, watching cars zip by, forlorn.

It is the land where a 4-year-old pre-schooler in Miami looks out his window and sees children on the streetside, blankets and clothes on the ground, begging for food.

What is unique about this pre-schooler is that he decides he must make a difference.

Joshua Williams went up to the older members of his large family- mother, six aunts, cousins, and grandmother- and told them he wanted to help the homeless people he saw around him.

They started cooking food for the homeless in the neighbourhood, distributing it each weekend.

"It starts as a passion or as a hobby, and what I loved to do was help others, make a difference, and put a smile on others' faces."

Soon, they were dedicating hours to this venture, and by the end of each week, they would have helped more than 200 people.

Suddenly, the child's dream and efforts to uplift those in need came crashing down.

"We had to stop this program because of a littering ordinance in Miami."

The end. Well, that was fast. Child feels, child dreams, child's heart is broken by reality.

That is until you get to the next part of the sentence: "But I wouldn't let that stop me."

His aunt (well, one of them) heard about 501(c)3s on the radio, the US act that provided for the founding of a tax-exempted, non-profit organisation- an NGO.

Thus was born the Joshua's Heart Foundation, an organisation which was exactly as it promised- created by Joshua's heart and kept going by his desire to help those less privileged than him.

Joshua's Heart has now expanded, reaching out far beyond the confines of his chest, home, and neighbourhood. It comforts the bodies of children with blankets and their tongues with the nourishing touch of food. Today, its reach extends from the US, Mexico and the Caribbean to India and the Philippines. It has distributed 2 million pounds of food and fed 450,000 people. It operates on the same principle as it did when it was a soup kitchen in the streets of Miami- distributing food. Now, of course, this isn't done by Joshua's small army of mom, grandma, and aunts, but by "mobile pantries"- community centres, churches, and schools.

Flyers are spread in the thousands to contact communities. "Community leaders" are sometimes selected, who help facilitate cooperation between Joshua's Heart and the aid recipients.

They stage massive events. Before an event, there is a flurry of printing and papers flapping in the wind days before the occasion, everyone flocking to take advantage of this display of precious resources. In the "first-come, first-serve" ones, there is a crowd of thousands gathering at the gate and demanding entrance, long lines streaming into the distance.

Back in Miami, Joshua's Heart gives those in need more than just food. They distribute food boxes and also emergency ones filled with toiletries and hygiene products.

A group of volunteers- a force of thousands- forays across Miami armed with these supplies, hand-delivering them to the homeless as they come.

We must remember where this revolution started. Not in a UNICEF office or in a conference room at Save the Children, not in the brain of some experienced social entrepreneur or the halls of a government department. It began with a kid who wanted to make a difference.

It began like this:

"There was one thing I knew I wanted to do: help others."

Our world would be better off if all of us looked at the blackest darkness and took away not fear or helplessness but a desire to bring some light into the lives of the afflicted. The way Joshua did. Our world would be better if all of us were so determined to do something so simple yet profound: helping others.

***

So where do we go for another such story? Do we travel thousands of miles, scrolling through a paltry list of teens for one that fits the bill?

We need not go far. For the young, action-driven teen is a common creature, hidden in a bedroom in every apartment, and with that initiative and aspiration often comes success and impact.

So in Florida itself, but in another corner of the swamp-infested, field-decorated landscape, lives Taylor Thigpen.

He is a 16-year-old school student.

Every day, when he went into the cafeteria at noon to eat his home-packed lunch, he saw 40% of his classmates who were otherwise kids just like him, friends he learned and played with, hungrily devouring the school's free lunch as if it were their first meal in days.

Some schools in the county, he knew, were even worse- 100% of their students were completely dependent on these free school meals for their sustenance, barely surviving.

But unlike the other students in the well-nourished 60% of his school, he took more than just pity and despondency from this situation.

"I hate to just talk about something," he says. "If I'm going to talk about it, I'm going to do it."

In his school cafeteria, all the children who got nutritious and complete meals did not wolf them down gratefully. Nearly half of their food would end untouched on the rack of plates. They wanted to play, they weren't hungry- how brilliant we humans are at coming up with reasons to not fully appreciate what we have.

It didn't feel right for there to be so much inequality, especially among students of the same school- some were heavily compromising, due to their income, on their diet, while others were piling their plates with quantities far beyond what they needed.

Surely that wasted food could be used by the 40% of children who didn't eat at home?

Thus was born the concept of the "share table". The concept is for students who don't eat packaged parts of their meals, such as fruit or milk, to drop them off at a table for others to take home. That way, more food is used, and the needs of disadvantaged students are fulfilled.

But fruit and milk weren't enough. The children needed something more substantial and essential to transforming their diet. So Thigpen approached the school faculty and began a vegetable growing campaign at school- fresh vegetables that students could take home.

In the garden, he also installed a compost bin where all cafeteria waste is used to enrich and enhance the garden's soil.

Thigpen saw hundreds of children taking advantage of the boost he had given them. He saw them becoming healthier, happier, and more active. But that was not enough.

He contacted his district superintendent and worked with his office to implement this program in 40 schools, impacting tens of thousands of students.

But Thigpen has bigger dreams. Florida is a large state, extending far beyond the confines of his district and county. He wants every school in the state to have share tables. So, having tested his idea at a grassroots level and kickstarted the initiative, he spends his evenings on the phone and email, ringing politicians, state senators, and the governor, to explain his endeavour and get their support. When the COVID-19 pandemic came and brought with it isolation, rather than insulating himself further, he saw it as a chance to help those in need, with the country brought to a standstill and much more free time on his hands.

The government and other organisations he contacted were very encouraging and keen to help out. He received $40,000 in grants and used that money to provide food boxes to 6,500 families in his county- boxes stacked with fruits, vegetables, meat, eggs, and milk.

Hours of his go away in such pursuits. People ask him about this schedule and bustle, and how he finds time for himself and "fun".

Such questions miss the point.

He has come to enjoy the activity of gardening and horticulture as a hobby, starting a small business- Succulent King- which sends cacti and succulents to all 50 American states. Some of the profits go to funding his hunger alleviation projects. This is an intriguing lesson- in stepping beyond our comfort zone to help others, we shine a light not just on others but on our own souls and our own paths. In the wide world, beyond our schools and homes and private interests, we discover our inner strengths and passions, and personalities.

But more importantly, he has come to cherish the feeling of having made a difference.

"I've seen kids go hungry, and I've had kids come up to me and say that I helped them eat tonight."

"If I decided to have fun instead of working every second of my life, that student may not have eaten that day."

Not a grandiose or elaborate quote from an eminent world leader or legend. But that, perhaps, is what makes it special. Because it comes from a real teenage hero. A kid like you or me.

YOUR GUIDE TO SAVING THE WORLD

All of us can learn from Joshua Williams and Taylor Thigpen. We can learn from them to replace ambivalence with care, inhibition with ambition, to "bring a smile to their faces", as Joshua said.

Clichéd? Perhaps that's how it sounds, but which do you prefer- the platitudes of those who watch from the sidelines or the action-oriented, positive words of those who step in to help?

For us to make a difference, what José taught us in Chapter 1 may be useful- curing the cause, not the symptoms.

Wasting less food in the first place is a very simple solution. Just leave less food on your plate at the end of your meal. We have all heard it at some point, perhaps from our parents, or our teachers in school. But few of us really implement the practice of not wasting food.

In India, 40% of all food is wasted. Let that sink in.

Now imagine you have taken three rotis, and you eat two of them. Does it sound outlandish now?

The reality is that all of us are contributing to the issue

without realising it, every day.

There are some simple solutions to this, provided by Social Value International:

- 💡 Control your portion sizes- do not take more food than you can eat.

- 💡 Do not always discard food just because it's past the "best-before" date on the packaging. Often, food will be good and safe to eat even after that date. Do your homework and check online or ask your parents if it could be safe to eat.

- 💡 Use leftovers from meals for another time or use them for making another dish. At my home, whenever anything is left over, for instance, especially a staple like rice or some vegetable, it is reused the next day.

- 💡 Also, trying homegrown food may not be a bad idea, like the vegetable garden in Thigpen's school. After all, not all food wastage occurs when you waste it while consuming it. Half of it happens in the production and transport stage. This waste too can be prevented by planting some vegetables and food at home, on the balcony, terrace, or garden, depending on the space available. My grandparents, for example, have a massive vegetable garden in their home in Delhi where everything from tomatoes to bitter gourd to brinjals is cultivated and then consumed.

- 💡 Joshua is far from alone. There are many organisations which allow the distribution of home-cooked food to others, and there is always the option of emulating him and serving meals to at least a few of the hungry and homeless on your own.

- 💡 Even raising awareness about it- asking your friends at lunchtime not to waste their food, or perhaps starting campaigns in your school with posters or on social media, could be valuable. Hardly anyone acts until the problem is thrust right in front of their faces.

As Mother Teresa said, "If you can't feed a hundred people, then feed just one." Millions around us are going hungry. There is no reason we cannot grow in ourselves a hunger to fight theirs, a hunger to bring relief and nutrition to them and a sense of achievement to us, much like Joshua and Taylor's happiness at being able to brighten the world of a child their age.

Virgil

"The greatest wealth is health"

Chapter 4

WELLBEING WARRIORS

2020. The year the world ended. A massive, world-changing pandemic shook our bliss of technological and medical security. We were not prepared. For all our safety nets and insulation, the pandemic did not flow on our shores like the tide but crashed upon them like a devastating tsunami.

Everything shut down.

Our lives shut down.

In June 2021, I had been in the US, on my summer holidays.

In June 2022, I was in bed, constantly incapacitated and weak, my thoughts and sight in a haze. I would erupt in vomiting whenever I consumed food more prepared, more complex, and more real, than puree and mashed porridge.

My mother and my father too fell sick- not with

COVID, but with other diseases, such as Dengue. But suffering knows no names and science- it knows only the pain it brings and the bodies it breaks.

At a time like this, shut off from everything outside my door, trapped in the tumults within, I felt like inside me was a void, a void of no warmth, light, or feeling. A cold, emotionless, prison, created by the disappearance of so many things I had taken for granted the first 12 years of my life.

A void I determined, pretty soon, I had to fill.

I stuck to what I knew I was good at and enjoyed- reading, writing books, practising Karate, making the most of the extra time with family at home, and connecting with grandparents through video calls.

I strove, day and night, to fill that space with positive things that gave me energy and fulfilment. But sometimes, I would wonder why COVID had affected me so much.

Was I so weak? Was a small change in circumstances all it took to make a mockery of all my pretensions of toughness and resilience?

Around the same time, I did a school project on preserving mental health and wellness during the pandemic.

Research told me I was not weak and I was not alone.

On May 29, 2020, thousands of Indian children and adolescents took a survey. They looked down at drab, fuzzily printed survey forms. "What were the emotions you felt the most during the pandemic?"

Worry- 60%. Helplessness- 57%. Anger- 52.2%. These were the alphas of the pack in the report compiled from this survey. Those were the beasts that tormented so many of us during those dire days.

When I speak to my friends today, nearly all of those with whom I discussed 2020 and '21 in passing refer to it as a time they'd prefer to forget, indeed sometimes wanting to act like it never happened.

"Mental health". I understand now that the phrase is more than just a Gen. Z buzzword. It represents a real concept, the health and resoluteness of our minds.

I was slightly surprised when, sometime last year, I learned that Good Health and Wellbeing was a UN SDG. The UN….that's an organisation for big things, right? Brokering peace between world powers, giving homes to refugees, building renewable energy infrastructure, saving ecosystems….stuff that, in massive ways, shapes the world.

I had never imagined the UN taking care of the health and state of mind of individuals- that was a job for psychiatrists and scientists, wasn't it?

But this SDG is more important than we think- if the people of this world can't be at peace within themselves, if they can't fix the tumults and torments in their own heads, how can we expect them to fix the world?

COVID also impacted physical health. By shutting us in our homes, it made children and adolescents 20% less physically active. Screen-time increased by 76% and 45% of children were spending more time on their laptops, compelled by online schooling, and 34% watched more TV to pass the time. Children and adolescents were becoming inactive, sinking further into the depths of already sedentary lifestyles.

This came forth in a deluge during COVID because it had been welling up against the dam of normal society and pastimes. These problems had existed and are core parts of the 21st-century world. COVID exacerbated these issues, but these had been growing for many years.

75% of teens are not getting the recommended amount of exercise, according to the University of Georgia. The average person spends more than 40% of his/her waking time on an internet screen. And there's worse. While fatigue softens the bones and screens scorch the eyes, smoke shrouds our lungs and alcohol eats away at our brains. 1 in 6 teens consumes tobacco, found a Centre for Disease Control and Prevention study.

These problems are not vague, ominous, mysteriously collecting and blackening the sky above. They live in our homes. Our choices breed them, and our habits feed them.

Solving them requires action every day from all of us, behind our walls and through them, in our minds and others. Like the other SDGs, this one may one day owe its fulfilment to us teens.

TEEN HEROES WHO ARE SAVING THE WORLD

Kisumu, Kenya. No, we are not in the Masai Mara or some grassland or wildlife reserve. We are in the third-largest city in the country. But here, too, there is beauty.

There is beauty in the view, as you stand upon a wooden plank extending in the air above the gently breaking waves of the sea, the amber evening sun splashing the sky with colours and gently colouring the blue, the crowns of trees silhouetted against the horizon.

There is beauty in the initiative of an 18-year-old, Michelle Oyoo Abiero, who has on this day determined in her heart to give solace and refuge to those out there like her who are bereaved and need support.

There is the deepest sorrow in the thoughts of her friend, who, five years earlier, confided in Michelle that she had been contemplating suicide. There was darkness in the path she was on, alone, leading to a destination where only death and loss for her loved ones awaited because she was afraid of taking help from or telling anyone else.

Something awoke in Michelle. She had seen how poor mental health could break people and lives, and she thought of the millions like her friend out there. At least her friend had had Michelle; there would be many without someone to lean on, to confide in and take strength from.

She focused initially on mental disorders, but as she has grown older and observed more and more issues around her, she expanded to bullying, body positivity, sexual assault, and unstable households.

The project leads mental health campaigns, hosts awareness campaigns and events provides resources and counselling and shares success stories to inspire. Hundreds of teenage Kenyans have availed Project Fmile's online therapy and support group.

Today, as you stand there beholding the sunset, find beauty not just in the natural spectacle but in the realisation that a 13-year-old girl stood up for the wellbeing of others in a country where three public hospitals take care of the mental health of 44 million citizens.

***

Alfie Regan is in front of the camera. Shirtless and in black shorts, there is a deflated, sullen expression on his face, eyes looking downwards as if trying to avoid the camera or studying his frame in the image.

He weighs 127 kg. He does not say "I am fat" or just shrug and say "it is what it is". He attributes his state to 18 years of bad choices. No exercise, lots of junk food- bad habits that have taken a heavy toll.

As he nears adulthood, he knows that continuing on this path will be a lifelong regret.

So overnight, he rejigs his entire schedule.

The time spent lazing and lounging in front of the television is replaced with working out- running, sports, going to the gym- everything that could quickly lift his body from its present state.

The mealtimes spent gorging on fast food and desserts vanish and are replaced with five meals- of protein snacks and drinks, to inject his body with much-needed vitality after 18 years of inactivity.

In one year, he has lost 45 kg. He now weighs just 82 kilograms, and when he stands in front of the camera he does so with a smile, proudly holding up a card recording his achievement.

But working on his own health does not satisfy him. He

wants to help others too, using the lessons he has learned during his amazing one-year journey.

He has started a 0-100 plan, aiming to help 100 people in Southampton become fitter. Not a massive movement online or using an app across the country- just personal work with people across the country, asking them to reach out to him for help via phone or email. When his friends, neighbours, and others congratulated him online, he felt like others like him deserved a chance too.

***

In the dark hours of the COVID Pandemic, while others around him were scrolling through Instagram or playing video games, there is a 16-year-old Indian boy wearing glasses, on a white sofa, legs crossed as he rests his back against a cushion. A book by Immanuel Kant is in his arms, as he peruses pages sharing perspectives on depression.

He slams the book shut. His eyes light up as if with the thrill of an epiphany, of a masterstroke of an idea. All those people in angst and depression due to the pandemic needed but one thing: a shift in perspective.

His name is Abhishek Krishnan. His classmate, Nihal Boina, has programming skills.

The two's ideas and strengths combine into Philio, an app creating personalised programs for users, filled with excerpts from philosophical works and activities designed to stimulate a change in users' perspective and invigorate their mental health.

Philio runs its course through the maze of the app store globally, lighting a spark in the lives of thousands, and spreading its glow all the way to Stanford University. The Department of Psychology at Stanford seizes on to it as exactly what it needed, recruiting the two teens as interns in the summer of 2021.

Krishnan's idea now advances, graduating from philosophical musing to psychological fact- exposure to philosophy improves mental health. So….prototyping? Check. Testing? Check. Validation? Check. Only one thing left: release.

They join a force of software engineers at Stanford and manifest the brewing storm of ideation and innovation into the creation of code and colours and screens and buttons.

Now Abhishek and Nikhil are more than contemplative teens gifted with a zeal for philosophy and technology; they had some of the best expert minds to consult, the most funding, and the most extensive resources in the world.

They launched it on the Google Play App Store, and it blazed away all opposition until it stood second in Medical Apps.

But unlike most apps, this success means much more than just a ranking on the App Store. This represents thousands of minds revitalised by the power of philosophy fused with modern medical science and the sheer dedication of two teens, who started off much like most of us- with a mere thought, a small connection made behind the pages of a book on a sofa somewhere.

YOUR GUIDE TO SAVING THE WORLD

More of us are like Krishnan than we imagine- sure, not all of us read profound works of philosophy, but many of us spend time thinking and introspecting without thinking of what we can really do to improve our mental health and that of others.

Here too, there are two aspects to taking action. One is taking care of yourself. To be healthy, there are several things you can do:

- 💡 Exercise. People who exercise 30 minutes a day on most days of the week have been 30% more likely to consider themselves happy than people who exercised much less. However, it does not always need to be vigorous or for long periods- even people who exercise ten minutes a day have been more buoyant and cheerful than people who exercise less. In the darkest days of COVID, practicing Karate at home kept me sane, not to mention fit.

- 💡 Find productive, constructive hobbies and passions. It is important to keep your mind occupied with hobbies or activities to keep developing yourself as a person and feel fulfilled, keeping you far away from stressful thoughts. For me, writing helps me not just express myself, but create a cocoon where I can focus on things that energise me, no matter what's happening in the world around me.

- 💡 Read a little. In one study at the University of Sussex, the stress of the subjects was reduced by 68% after just 6 minutes of reading. Also, regular readers sleep better and have lower stress levels, higher self-esteem, and lower rates of depression. Writing anything from a diary, or a blog as a hobby can significantly increase happiness and decrease stress levels.

- 💡 Spend quality time with others- family, and friends. According to the findings of a research study published in *the Journal of Epidemiology and Public Health*, family rituals and quality time with parents correlate with improved mental health and fewer delinquent behaviours among adolescents.

Apart from this, like Alfie did, like Michelle with her friend who was considering suicide, help out your family and friends with any issues they are facing like Alfie did- related to physical fitness or mental health, using some of these tips and looking at their current habits and circumstances. Giving the smallest boost to someone feeling low is beneficial for you too. It makes you happy, boosting your mood and well-being. According to Psychiatrist Dr. Francoise Adan, director at University Hospitals in Cleveland, *"Being happy doesn't just make us feel better, it improves our health. It helps us eat healthier, be more active and sleep better."*

That's the full circle. Help yourself, then help others and, in doing so, help yourself again. Perhaps that's what this book is all about.

WB Yeats

"Education is not the filling of a pail, but the lighting of a fire"

Quality Education

Chapter 5

EDUCATION ELECTRIFIERS

Every day, I would go to school at 7:30 in the morning, board the bus, and return home at 4:30 after nine hours of travelling, doing classes, playing, and chatting with friends. I would return to meet my mother in the living room, and we would chat about the day.

One day, I came back, and she told me she had begun volunteering for Angel Xpress, teaching Maths and English to kids from slums. She went every day in the late morning to a temple where Angel Xpress had set up one of their centres, where the kids they served would come to learn from teachers such as my mother.

My mom told me, "They do not go to very good schools like yours, and don't come from very well-off families. It's not just what we teach them that matters, but the fact that they get exposure to different people, people who can help them think of doing something very different with their lives, something possible only through education."

I used to chat sometimes with her about the classes and heard stories- children up to mischief, each with a different story and background and situation at home, which would shine through at times. They struggled with some parts of English, but many were resilient and were completely dedicated to learning and stretching themselves. They would ask my mother about her life too. Once, she showed them a picture of me, and they got excited to think that she had a son of around their age. I was in Goa, on a beach, a world very distant from them, many of whom had never gone beyond Mumbai.

Hearing of my mother's work at Angel Xpress was a more powerful reminder than any lecture, video, article, or school lesson that not everyone has access to the same opportunities that I do.

50% of Indian children 6-18 do not currently go to school. Around a third of them have never been to school. And a sixth of them are working.

We say that education builds our futures, but the majority of the students that do attend school don't know how important it can be to unlocking their future and a big difference is played by the kind of environment they grow up in.

A study published in the *Oxford Review of Education* found that less privileged students agreed 14-17 said twice as many times that they were unlikely to apply to university than more privileged students of the same age and with the same test scores.

TEEN HEROES WHO ARE SAVING THE WORLD

When I think of a hero who is doing something to help in the effort to provide education to others, I don't have to look far. In my school, there is a girl named Shivani Shrotri. She is in Grade 12 and whenever I pass her in the corridor or the staircases on campus, I think of how here, right in front of me, is someone like the other teen changemakers I've written about in this book, who has done the sort of thing that gets people written about and widely acclaimed for the positive impact they've had on society.

An avid debater in Speech Debate India, she was debating in late 2019 on a plan to improve the educational system.

From that debate, she did not take away just an academic understanding of education in India and the nuances of setting up a new system. She took something more from the experience.

There was a colossal disparity between the education that many receive. "Something sparked within me", she said. "It was just so sad to me and it felt so unfair to me that just because of something that's not even the student's fault they're at a disadvantage."

With technology changing the way education can be imparted and making possible access to information and resources that was unthinkable just a few decades ago, students going to school with access to such technology often have a great advantage over those going to schools that cannot afford, or do not have access to, such technology.

This was particularly visible during the pandemic.

Only 39% of children said they were likely to receive remote education and 36% of Indian children had no internet access, so their learning completely stalled in 2020-21 when all schools relied on online learning. Even those who had some internet access, were at a disadvantage because they didn't have the bandwidth or infrastructure to attend online Zoom classes, like more privileged kids. The maid at my home used to tell us about how her daughter was learning through WhatsApp- the schools would send worksheets and videos to work on and watch, and she had to learn and keep up, with virtually no live interaction with her teachers.

Shivani said in an interview.

"Now that the pandemic has forced classes online, they [the underprivileged students] shouldn't be at a disadvantage".

"I've been so inclined towards the STEM subjects like Science, Math, and Computer Science."

She decided to use this strength of hers to share her skills and knowledge with underprivileged children.

During the COVID pandemic, when her target audience was so frustratingly out of reach, she started a YouTube channel, filling it with educational videos on coding.

As she dove deeper into the issue, she realised there was more to it than hardware inaccessibility. There was no system for teaching computer skills. No government standardised curriculum.

She could not set up a factory and start manufacturing

cheap laptops and distributing them across the country.

She did not have massive capital, resources, or funding. But she had knowledge of the skills needed (from coding classes), the way the children's minds worked (from school Psychology classes), and the issue she wanted to deal with.

So, she made a curriculum- a plan, month-by-month, session-by-session, for teaching underprivileged kids coding.

After a few months of research, ideation, and revision, she was done. But for any student to use her work, she had to be something more than a conscious, smart teenager with a few ideas typed on her laptop.

She would have to become a leader, a leader of an organisation and movement, to get noticed and make a real impact on bridging the digital divide.

She would be the founder and CEO of Gen Z. Codes, an NGO that aspired to bring the skills of the information age to children across the country and pave the way to a more equitable tomorrow.

Shivani emailed dozens of social organisations focused on children. Every day, she would send emails, dogged in her persistence. At last, she got a reply. Smile Foundation, an NGO with education centres all over India, was interested in working with her. Shivani lit up the moment she saw their response. These centres were perfect places for Gen Z. Codes to come to life.

Her school nominated her for the IB Social Innovator's Award, an award given by the IB to social innovation projects. With the award came recognition, fame, and

USD 7,000 of funding.

"Surprisingly, I got it", she says, laughing, as she stands in the front of my classroom. She has been asked by my teachers to narrate her story, and inspire us for our upcoming individual service projects. To see someone I know become part of the war to save the world was electrifying.

Thus was, truly, born Gen Z. Codes. It joined forces with Angel Xpress and a horde of other NGOs, and, a year after Shivani first sat down with her laptop, has 300+ students.

Gen Z. Codes has branched off into numerous other movements that do everything, from teaching the elderly digital literacy to equipping women newly arrived from the darkness of human trafficking or domestic abuse with the skills they require to reinvigorate their lives and leave behind the past.

On YouTube, its channel continues to flower, blooming into a beautiful creation of unforeseen proportions. More than 100,000 students have seen Shivani's videos, overcoming boundaries of birth, time, and space, to absorb the expertise needed to succeed in today's digital world.

Shivani was a 14-year-old armed with a laptop, basic coding skills, and ambition when she began. Now, she stands higher than most educated, qualified adults in her impact on the digital literacy of children. Sure, the supporting organisations helped, but what made the difference was her willingness and courage to step up and do her bit.

***

2019. It is July 30- Friendship Day. With my friends, it is a fairly simple affair- some of us tie friendship bracelets for each other. Perhaps there are others who spend extra time with friends on these days, going out with them, enjoying their time together.

Sukriti Chiripal, a grade 11 girl in Kolkata, is standing in a black t-shirt, with a white circle at the centre and "Sangam" scrawled in italics within. She is in a broad, rectangular room with off-white walls and a television attached to the wall. On the floor are seated dozens of children, in small circles that mingle with each other to give the impression of a room of friends sharing something. From underneath them is visible a few yards of yellow carpets embroidered with designs in red, curling gently in the tendrils of plants and the whorls of flowers. The children are bent, giving the impression that they are doing something purposefully and with great concentration. Before them are notebooks, ruled pages neatly connected with spiralled binding.

They are doing a workshop called "Trash to Treasure", in which the students are recycling used exercise activities to create new ones, and together revelling in fun learning activities. The positivity flowing in the room sure does give Friendship Day vibes.

But how did we get here? Who is the girl standing in the room, and what is Sangam?

One day, a few street children came to Sukriti for a donation. She asked them why they weren't in school, and they told her that their parents didn't think it worthwhile. She was astounded and noticed over time that the problem was even bigger for girls than boys.

She started doing something few of us would have dared, visiting the families of the children and convincing them to let their kids attend school.

Initially, they walled her out, seeing her as a dangerous influence on their sons and daughters. But over time, as she went to them bearing books, and articles from another world, they were more easily persuaded.

Inspired by this, she started Sangam, an initiative with a few friends that aimed to collect books and stationery to facilitate the education of the underprivileged.

In one major drive in 2018, they collected 600 books, benefiting scores of underprivileged children.

Her parents stood by her, never dissuading her or looking at it pessimistically and concluding that the issue was bigger than her.

Back to Friendship Day, when we started: Sangam has 50 volunteers and has grown into a nationwide movement working in Mumbai, Delhi, Pune, Kolkata, Bangalore, and Raipur.

"We want to support the education of as many underprivileged children as possible", she tells a Times of India interviewer who is looking in through the door of her room, intrigued. She will push on, and her efforts will continue shining a light on the lives of dozens of kids in need, just as her persistence uplifted the first underprivileged kids whose parents she spoke to when Sangam wasn't even born.

YOUR GUIDE TO SAVING THE WORLD

Shivani and Sukriti are two girls who battled, by their standards and the standards of an ever-changing world, ancient and deep-rooted societal and cultural issues- the economic and technological inequalities that shape our most basic conception of society, and the discouraging attitudes to schooling among lower-income families.

But they stood tall, stuck with their innermost feelings about the problem, and pushed on to give better education to those formerly denied it.

There are many simple things we can do to help.

The way I see it, there are two approaches to contributing to the cause- one is supporting large NGOs and organisations, with enormous reaches across cities and states, and the other is looking at the community around you and seeking to help it. Shivani took the first, Sukriti the second, and both succeeded in having a meaningful impact.

Look at old books, stationery, etc, you may have and donate them to NGOs who can pass them on to kids in need. There are many such organisations- Goonj, Smile Foundation, and smaller regional or intra-city ones.

Observe the situation of children in your neighbourhood, or perhaps the children of your household, and see whether you can support them in any way. You could help them with education, teaching them any subjects or skills depending on their academic situation and curriculum at school. In addition, you could give them some of your textbooks to help them study. My family has done this, donating some used or old textbooks to my driver's and maid's families, and they have always been grateful if it matches their child's needs, and seen them use the material to good effect.

Malala Yousafzai- now there's a (former) difference-making teenager who needs no introductions- once said "One child, one teacher, one book, and one pen can change the world".

This seems a very apt quote for this book that claims to be the guide to "Saving the world". Without education, and optimal learning, underprivileged kids are essentially incapacitated, with no knowledge for guidance on succeeding in the world and rising above their humble beginnings. We aren't discussing transforming ecosystems or political systems or recalibrating society- just helping out some fellow teens and kids who need support. If Shivani and Sukriti could make a difference, two teens with no real unique expertise or resources most of us don't have, we can too.

Malala Yousufzai

"We cannot all succeed when half of us are held back."

Chapter 6

GENDER EQUALITY GALVANIZERS

Once, I was playing Cricket with friends near my home, in the wide, green, park just in front of my building. A girl came up to us. "Can I play with you guys?" One of my friends laughed. "Girls can't play. Only boys are playing here." A few others chorused in approval, and she left, irritated and angry.

I have always been a Cricket fanatic, fervently following all matches, from domestic leagues and the IPL to the World Cups, and have especially followed the Indian men's cricket team. This incident, though, made me think about the other half of humanity- women, and girls.

Why had I seen such little media coverage on them in the sport, so few fans of Mithali Raj and Smriti Mandhana while people chanted the names of Kohli and Dhoni and wore their jerseys?

Almost no women's matches were broadcasted, except for the World Cups and some key Indian matches. Even series like the Women's Ashes, whose male counterpart is received with much fanfare, was never shown on TV.

The prize money for winning the Women's World Cup is 2 million dollars, compared to 4 million for the Men.

Until late October 2022, when BCCI and several other international cricket boards equalised men's and women's pay, there was a staggeringly massive gulf between women's and men's pay in cricket. Grade A women's cricketers, the best of them, were paid 50 lakh Rupees, compared to between Rupees 1-7 crore for all men's cricketers. This was attributed to men's cricketers playing a higher number of games.

When this episode took place, I was just eight, so cricket was very naturally my door to exploring the wider issue. Over the last six years, as I have built knowledge and understanding of the pressing nature of gender inequality, I have grown more and more concerned.

According to the Centre for Global Development, women are 12.5% more likely to be denied formal education. They are denied the opportunities and support they need to prosper, which is why they frequently bear the brunt of issues like poverty and struggle more than men.

Men earn 22% more than women- a dollar for every 82 cents women earn.

In the US, women are 35% more likely than men to be afflicted by poverty. 60% of all chronically hungry people are women.

We all know about gender equality and women empowerment and feminism. These are big words, and sometimes we run the risk of just watching Ted talks, and staging academic discussions- paying lip service to these concepts, rather than really understanding the problem and trying our best to tackle it.

Turns out, if we lend our voices and actions to solving gender equality, we can all have an impact.

***

I have been learning Karate since I was in Grade 1, since 2015. Besides enjoying the classes with their tough routines of exercise, discipline, and then sparring, I always noticed one thing- the conspicuous absence of girls in our classes. The vast majority of students were boys, and that ratio became even more lopsided when I looked at the senior students.

When I received my Black Belt in 2019, only one of the five students who got their Black Belt with me in my class was a girl.

Loving Karate, I had read a lot about its benefits and knew about its potential to empower everyone.

In a University of Oregon study, 80% of participants in a martial arts class underwent increased self-esteem.

Women are also equipped with self-defence skills through martial arts and confidence in their safety- an organisation called Model Mugging which teaches women martial arts found that 1% of their students were assaulted versus 33% of women globally.

A University of Nebraska study found that learning martial arts for just 8 months improved academic attitude by 85%, self-esteem by 29%, and social attitude by 22%.

Surely girls deserved these benefits? Why then, were there so few in my class?

I decided to conduct a survey among parents, both in my Karate class and my building and neighbourhood, to understand the barriers. The divergence in the parents' ways of thinking became very evident:

- 48% of boys' parents reported their child was learning martial arts compared to 21% of girls' parents.

- 21% of girls dropped out of martial arts classes, versus 10% of boys.

- 76% of boys' parents said there were no barriers to their child studying martial arts, compared to just 21% of girls' parents.

- 58% of girl parents said they didn't enrol their children due to the risk of injury. Just 16% of boys' parents had this fear.

- 37% of girls' parents said their children were completely disinterested in martial arts, far more than 16% of boys' parents.

I felt glad to, at last, have some of the mystery unravelled, the issue crystalised into data and insights that gave me hints into what could be done to solve the issue.

I used my intuition to draft a list of solutions to each of the barriers and problems involved that barred girls from attending martial arts classes as much as boys.

It sounds simple and logical, but, as a quote I used at the beginning of the book went, "Words are just words until you bring them to life".

I thought of the realities at my Karate dojo and the Federation that ran it, and how those could be changed to overcome these obstacles. I also interviewed my Sensei to get his perspective and a better picture of what the Federation was doing.

One idea I had was to make full safety equipment mandatory and communicate that to parents and girls. Kids used gloves while sparring, but a lot of Karate safety equipment such as chest guards, shin guards, and head guards, were not mandatory, amplifying both the actual and perceived risk of injury.

Another was only doing weapons training for older kids or keeping it optional. Weapons training with wooden knives and wooden sticks was mandatory, which my Sensei told me put off many girls' parents.

I also thought of using social media to get more girls interested. The Federation used seminars and shows at festivals and posters put around societies, which are less relevant in today's age when most young people discover ideas on social media and online.

Moreover, even when Instagram was used it was for posting about teachers and championships. The testimonies and visuals of female students and teachers would make the content more relevant to girls and their parents, and use ethos (credibility) as those photos would undoubtedly be more credible advertisements for the Federation.

I created a report with these and sent it to the teachers at the Federation, including my Sensei. I received a very positive response to my findings and suggestions, with many saying they had never thought of these suggestions even though they were fairly simple.

I was happy to have made a start in dealing with the issue in a setting and community I was a part of, playing a role in optimising the classes for the girls and their parents so they could avail the benefits of Karate.

That was as rewarding as the day I earned my Black Belt.

TEEN HEROES WHO ARE SAVING THE WORLD

There is a village in Bangladesh. Thatched huts shining in the sun, in a lush, humid, verdant forest, overlooking a vast wetland of algae beds floating tranquilly upon deep blue water, stretching till the horizon, with groups of farmers plucking stalks of rice from the waters.

Beautiful, but it's also the place where the ugly reality of child marriage exists. It's the place where several young boys, with their parents, gathered around the home of a 12-year-old girl, asking for her hand in marriage.

The place where the girl's mother had been married at

the age of 13 to a 21-year-old man, and when asked by her daughter to share childhood stories and memories, came up blank due to the early marriage and the resumption of a premature adult life of marriage, barring her from her interests and becoming someone in her own right.

According to UNICEF, 59% of girls in Bangladesh marry before they turn 18.

But not this girl.

Dola Akter Reba had a very different destiny, driven by her desire to do something greater, and her fury at the injustice her mother and friends had suffered, at the brazenness of society in shoehorning young girls into rearing families from such a young age.

She staunchly refused. And somehow, perhaps because of her resolve, her mother saw something of the hope and resistance that she held dear as a torchlight in the darkness after her own experiences, and she escaped becoming an outcast or a worse fate.

Saving herself from child marriage, though, was not enough. Reba was on a new path now, and there was no going back.

She joined the organization World Vision. When she became part of one of its "child forums", she was allowed to engage with a family from another village through a child forum. She was persistent even when the parents spoke to her about the importance of tradition, of continuing the bloodline and making sure that their daughter fulfilled her role of giving birth to healthy children after marrying.

Armed with her experiences, and the preparation she got from World Vision, she spoke to them at length, not as a lecturer or disposer of enlightenment or knowledge but as an equal who understood their dilemmas and circumstances and wanted to help them and their daughter.

Their daughter turned 18 a while later, and she was not married.

That was her first victory, but by no means her last.

That was how, by the time she turned 16 four years later, Reba, with the help of her close colleagues, had prevented 600 child marriages.

In 2021, she was invited to speak at the UN in Geneva about her work and communicate to the international community from the depths of her heart and the heights of her success the importance of the issue and acting on it.

All of this, begun by one teen's willpower and dream.

YOUR GUIDE TO SAVING THE WORLD

Imagine if the boys who had stopped the girl from playing with us that summer day in 2016 had let her come and join us. She would have felt uplifted, motivated, and equal to us. It would have been one small deed, but it would have given her more confidence, made her feel included, and made us boys start to take off some of the blinkers which distorted our vision of what girls could do or not do.

Many, nearly all of us, are guilty of propagating gender stereotypes in one way or another. I have heard many of my friends and classmates commenting on girls in close-minded and derogatory terms. I plead guilty to at times not questioning gender stereotypes and disparities around me, taking them for granted.

Each one of us can make a difference, and it starts by changing our minds. But issues like gender inequality are built by societies, by the combined force of millions of minds. Each of those needs to change, feel the need to do something different if we are to ever create a more equal world for women and girls.

So, in your daily life, do not, even casually, do or say anything that is based on our myths as a society regarding women's capabilities. That is the least we can do to create a more compassionate and equitable atmosphere.

There, of course, is a wider arena for action on gender equality. Depending on the reality in our immediate surroundings, we can do our best to stimulate women's empowerment and gender equality. I saw the gender gap in my Karate class, so that is where I took action. Gender inequality isn't hard to find, so there must be some settings in your life too where you see it run rampant and compromise the self-esteem and success of the girls involved. Whether on the playground, in our classes, or in our neighbourhoods, we will find opportunities to make a difference. We are growing up in a very different generation, where we are encouraged to create a more empathetic and inclusive world, one that is blind to the stereotypes of the past. However, the choice is ours, do we create the world we want, the world we will inherit as adults, or do we go with the flow and accept the world as it has been created, poisoned by past stereotypes?

Volunteering for NGOs is another option- something like what Reba did. Many organisations give opportunities for working with them to support disadvantaged girls socially or educationally. Donating to these NGOs would certainly be helpful too. The organization Reba joined- World Vision- for example, was completely driven by donations.

Change does happen, and each of us can make a little difference. I took a very small step at my dojo, Reba took a giant leap in her community, and slowly, and surely, change is happening.

Oh, and as I write this book, the first season of the Women's Premier League is kicking off, women cricketers are getting many of the opportunities their male colleagues have taken for granted, and in the sport that I love so much, we are starting to see some signs of gender equity. My favourite cricketer is Virat Kohli, who wears jersey number 18 for the Royal Challengers Bangalore team. This year, I'll be cheering equally vociferously for another maestro who will wear the same jersey number for the same team- Smriti Mandhana.

Audrey Hepburn

"Water is life, and clean water means health."

Chapter 7

WATER WARRIORS

Very frequently, at least once every couple of days, upon entering the school washroom, I see a tap running. Someone has used it recently and forgotten to shut it, and even in the seconds or microseconds I watch it before stopping it, it flows continuously into the drain, unused.

Then I imagine a parched, thirsty throat, dried out in the midst of the Sahara Desert, and all that water pouring down that throat. To the person with that throat, this would be a life saviour. To me, it is a mere footnote in a day packed with other less essential and more "important" things. After all, water is the least of my personal concerns.

Once, at school, in Grade 2, I think, we were asked to make a poster on water wastage, raising awareness of the issue and encouraging people not to take part in it. I remember it, with a picture of the Earth at the centre, an unshapely circle drawn with my not-so-artistic hand, and the upside-down curve of a sad face drawn on it. I surrounded it with facts and statistics and calls to action about the problem of water scarcity and how it was killing our planet and endangering us.

70% of the planet is covered by water, but only 2.5% of it is freshwater. 99% of this is locked in glaciers and snowfields.

So only 0.007% of Earth's water is available for all of humanity.

And even this is fast disappearing. The whole world may face a severe water shortage by 2040.

1.1 billion people lack water access, and 2.7 billion are short on it at least 1 month a year.

Suddenly, I looked at the drinking water that filled my bottle, the tap water flowing from my sink, and the polluted river water filled with sludge struggling through the narrow spaces in Mumbai, differently, with less ambivalence and more sadness and concern.

That is how I came upon this issue. For a long time, I have been turning off taps when I don't need them, but have still felt sorry for not being able to do more for the water crisis our world is facing. When I take a hearty drink from a bottle of water, I savour its pure taste, wondering how soon the sensation will be lost to history.

Without water, we are nothing. Some world we teens are inheriting!

Thankfully, here too, some have stood forth and done something to preserve this precious, life-giving resource.

Those of our age who have shown others the way to avoiding the rapid, irreversible loss of water and inspire us to take action.

TEEN HEROES WHO ARE SAVING THE WORLD

Israel. That word conjures images of a small desert, barren, nation holding its own against the war and instability that surrounds it. For the more historically minded of us, it makes us think of Jerusalem, the holy city for Christianity, Islam, and Judaism, with the Dome of the Rock and the Crusades.

It is 2011. Desert storms rage, as the soil is parched and cracks emerge in the ground, as millions are dehydrated, in a truly apocalyptic series of events.

The country panics. It is on the brink of catastrophe. Advertisements come out en masse, featuring famous singers and actors. In one of them, a woman with drying, cracking, flaky skin, looks at the camera forlornly, with deathly pale eyes. "Israel is dying out", she says.

Over the next two years, everyone works hard. Governments build better supply lines. In homes and offices, people turn off taps and showers and sparingly use the toilet like their life depends on it.

And in dozens of schools across the country, an army of thousands of students is toiling.

On the roof of their schools, they are creating and maintaining massive tanks and containers of concrete and plastic. Every day during the monsoon, hundreds of thousands of raindrops fall into each of these, before an attached mechanism filters this and sends it to be used.

Each time someone goes to check on it, and the water flowing into the product of his hard work washes away all misgivings as the student realises that he or she has done something good for the future of the nation.

A few months earlier, people from an organisation called Green Horizon had come to the school to raise awareness of the water crisis- as if that needed any awareness-spreading- and the concept of rainwater harvesting.

The next few months were spent in a rush of planning and discussion and manufacturing, as the children seized upon this novel opportunity to join the war against drought and water shortage, and the death of Israel.

"Students are inspired by learning that they can do more than just turn off taps- they can save an entire season's worth of rain", said an employee of Green Horizon.

Come 2013. The ads are no longer on television. No one is talking about Israel's doom and the dehydrated masses. Not because the struggle has sucked all the hope and fight from the populace and its leaders, but because Israel has triumphed.

Today, it recycles more water than any other nation- 80%, compared to 30% in India and 10% in the US, for instance. It is basking in glory, the cooling, comforting shade made by its empowered, persistent children and teens to shield Israel from the scorching sun and climate change for a little longer.

***

Farmland. California. Stalks of wheat flutter in the wind. Cattle munch idly on the grass nearby, hills and valleys meandering into the verdant distance.

A farmer, a middle-aged chap in rough earthen, natural colours of brown and green and dark blue. A red, cylindrical truck is in front of the tree. Amongst the text on it is "Water tanker".

The farmer frowns, and it seems like there is more than the sunlight that is bugging him. He is talking to a 10-year-old girl named Shreya Ramachandran.

"My well has gone completely dry", he says. "I have no water in my home. My wife, my daughter, me- we have nothing."

"How do you survive?"

"Water tankers bring water here from better-endowed parts." He shoots a sunken look and a sigh at the water tanker.

Eight years later, Shreya is standing against a backdrop of cars and traffic lights and shop placards and edifices. There is a reporter, a tall man in a grey suit and tie, in front of her, and another holding a camera.

"I was really affected by their stories, and I wanted to do something to help."

Ramachandran's home in Fremont, California, was a good distance away from the farm she'd been to in 2014. But the farmer's plight told her one thing: the water crisis was closer to home and more real than she believed.

She came back to Fremont. The next day, she stood, mouth open and all teeth showing, furiously scrubbing away with a toothbrush. The tap was off.

In the shower, she was out in five minutes, not fifteen.

But this was not enough. Nothing seemed to have changed. It probably should have. It may have. But it wasn't good enough; there was no evidence.

One day, she stood just outside her bathroom, and she saw two smooth, brown-shelled fruits, and one yellow fruit. The previous day, her grandmother had boarded the plane from Fremont to Chennai. She had stayed for five days, and on the first had told Shreya that those nuts had been traditionally used in India for bathing.

"Massage one in a bowl of lather until it smells strongly of apples. Then it is ready."

She took one and soon prepared a bowl foaming with a white mass of soap water, and it worked. For days, she used the nuts as shampoo. One day, the fragrance of apples floated down her nostrils, and dreamlike thoughts and visions seeped through the nebulous cloud of her awakening mind. Suddenly, there was a jolt, like a trembling of the Earth, and the mist dissipated. In its place was a thought. The germ of an idea that would change her life.

Soap nuts as laundry detergent. Litres of reused water.

She went to her kitchen with a stack of 30-40 clothes, put 3-4 in the machine, mixed them with water prepared with the soap nuts, and let the machine do its work. After some time, she would come with three more garments and put them in, and repeat 8 more times, until the soap nuts stopped working.

So the same water could be reused 10 times, and the

same nuts, all without using detergent. That stray spark of her imagination created something new.

Simple, intuitive, seemingly unscientific. But Shreya was not prepared to let it remain that way. She wanted the world, the scientific community, to know and recognise her invention. Besides, how much difference did five nuts in one washing machine make? Then she thought, how much would five thousand nuts in a thousand homes?

But for this thought to come to anything, she had to step up. Step up from the whirring of a washing machine and the wetness of soap; graduate to the cavernous halls of universities and the bustling, tangled world of research. The first stage was complete. The washing machine had given her many answers. Now, it was the academia's turn.

For hours, she scrolled through thousands of pages of graphs and abstracts and hypotheses. The idea became a plan. A plan for a project: The Grey Water Project, the eponymous Grey Water being the water reused with the soap nut detergent.

How great it would be, she mused, if she'd been in the place of one of the researchers, one of the authors and investigators in the research papers and experiments she read.

Yes, that was it. She needed one of them for help. They were everywhere, from the coast to the prairies, and she knew that. Time for some emails.

Time for dozens of emails and days spent eyeing her inbox and sending mail, her requests unheard. But she did not lose hope. All she needed was to catch one person's eye, and get one kind reply.

She awoke one day, bleary-eyed and nose full of the scent of apples from her bath when there was a beep.

"Celind Pallud", it said. She opened it. "Soil Scientist at University of California, Berkeley."

"Your experiments are extremely impressive", the message said, "Comparable to the work of a college student. I will look over it and greenlight it."

That was the beginning. The beginning of the beginning. Grey Water was to prove a real powerhouse in water conservation in the year to come.

With the labs of the University and her steely resolve and ever-analysing brain, she founded an NGO- the Grey Water Project.

She made science curriculums and spoke at schools, libraries, and offices. Word and appreciation of her work had spread to 90 American schools by 2020.

From a stroke of inspiration in her home, she had created a much bigger impact than she might have ever imagined possible.

YOUR GUIDE TO SAVING THE WORLD

These two case studies have it all- inspirational stories of resolve and determination in dealing with the water crisis, and lessons on the practical steps that optimise such efforts.

The most basic level of the solutions to conserve water is the kind adopted initially by Shreya:

💡 Turn taps off after using it and while doing something

else, such as brushing your teeth.

- 💡 Use artificial dishwashers less and hand-wash dishes with soap more. The machines waste significant quantities of water.

- 💡 Place some limit on the time you spend in the shower. These, quite obviously, use a lot of water, and every minute less taken to bathe using these is valuable.

The next is adopting more advanced solutions, like the ones both case studies eventually went for.

Think of methods to conserve water, such as rainwater harvesting or Shreya's "grey-water" technique. You can work at your school or home to set up infrastructure like rainwater harvesters or implement smaller-scale fixes too.

Being an active water conservationist in your daily life, and by extension in the life of your community, requires concern, innovation, and work.

So the next time you are washing your hands, remember what Benjamin Franklin said: "When the well is dry, we'll know the worth of water."

The well will dry up soon. In washing your hands, in taking a bath, in taking every sip from your bottle, you are drawing water from that well. Make sure to draw it sparingly, or it will dry up soon. Then we will all know the worth of water. We will crave it, be ready to die for it- but it will not come.

Thomas Alva Edison

"I'd put my money on the Sun. What a source of power! I hope we don't have to wait till oil and gas run out till we tackle that!"

Chapter 8

ENERGY EXEMPLARS

Like many other kids, I was always fascinated by dinosaurs. I would read books, play with toys, and spend a lot of my waking time immersed in the prehistoric world when scaled, winged, clawed, sharp-toothed beasts walked the Earth and ruled the seas, against a magnificent backdrop of volcanoes and ginkgo trees and wide plains undiscovered by man. I knew the names of nearly every dinosaur, from Stegosaurus, T-rex, and Triceratops to Argentinosaurus, Rajasaurus, Brontosaurus, Maiasaurus, Spinosaurus…. you name it.

Every day, in the morning before school, I would search for videos of mock dinosaur battles and analyses of whether Stegosaurus could beat T-rex.

As the years passed, I learned in school about fossil fuels- energy sources like coal, oil, and natural gas- and how they were taken by mining fossils, the bony remnants of the dinosaurs deep underground in sea-beds or soil. I was amazed. So the living matter of the dinosaurs was still, 66 million years later, powering our existence and the working of our societies and economies?

However, over time, disturbing realities emerged that threatened to destroy my simple childlike awe of fossil fuels- emissions, greenhouse gases, and global warming. It became very clear soon that the whole world wants to move on from them, and sees them only as a temporary substitute for future technologies- "renewable energy".

In school, we learned about green energy, and I researched in-depth about wind power and solar power. what struck me is that we were so late in the race to save ourselves from climate change. Even as organisations like the UN say we have only a few more years, we are in the prototyping stage, with thousands of people coming up with outlandish, conflicting ideas without narrowing down on the best ones. I dismissed them a little, as distant things, hopeful, well-meaning fantasies that weren't really working. Sure, some statistics said more people were using them, and their cost was reducing, but I didn't see any building in my city powered by renewable energy- neither mine nor my friend's nor office buildings or malls.

That all changed when last year, my dad told me that he had just gotten our house powered by 100% Green Power, an initiative launched through the energy company supplying electricity to our building, where we could switch to sustainable energy sources at a slight additional cost. I realised that things like renewable energy were not only things that lay in the province of textbooks and large government projects, but something individuals could make choices on and act on in, and close to, their homes.

TEEN HEROES WHO ARE SAVING THE WORLD

Nepal. The beautiful, northern border country of India is dotted with snow-capped peaks, lush, green valleys, and dark brown vales of rock and sediment.

It is 2005. Milan Karki is a 14-year-old boy. His village stands in the shadow of a towering cliff, a hill of rock and soil raised up towards the sky.

The shadow it cast on the homes only further amplified their darkness- for 16 hours a day, there was not a single lightbulb, motor, or machine in the entire settlement, not a volt of electricity flowing through the wires.

Milan was from a relatively high-income family, so he went to school and was exposed to science and knowledge of the work of great inventors like Thomas Edison, whom he made his idol. He was reading a book by Stephen Hawking, discussing ways of creating static electricity from hair.

That's when he realised that Melanin can be used to convert energy- to electrical energy.

Melanin was perfect. It was cheap, essential in a country like Nepal and indeed any country in the making of feasible, easy-to-implement solutions. Half a kilo of hair can be bought for 16 *paisa* in Nepal and last months, while a pack of batteries costs 50 *paisa* and lasts just a few nights.

A solar panel made of Melanin instead of Silicon could do wonders for the village. He tried to convince the villagers, but they were sceptical.

"They believe in superstitions, they don't believe in science", Milan says.

So he and four classmates set out to prove them wrong. They were at work for many months on end, manufacturing something completely unprecedented in the history of power generation. But eventually, they managed it.

Some were sent out to the districts for testing feasibility, and demonstrations have persuaded the villagers of their utility. "Now they believe", says Milan.

Each panel produces 9 volts of energy, and the cost will only reduce as it is mass-produced. Milan says they could be sold for half the current price once they become common enough. Within just a few years, he was dreaming of spreading his invention far and wide, to other cities, even other nations. Everyone could do with cost-effective, sustainable solutions, not just Nepalis.

"First I wanted to provide electricity for my home, then my village. Now I am thinking for the whole world", said Milan.

***

It is 2014. Ethan Novek is on the beach, the afternoon sun blazing on his skin and the sand on the seashore. He has a shovel, and with that is scraping away at the sand, digging a hole. Over the next half-hour, he observes the hole filling up, the blackness inside nearly completely inhabited by water welling up to the brim. As the tide rose and the waves crashing on the shoreline a few feet away gained force, the water level increased steadily.

What if, he thinks, there was a way to capture the natural energy in these rising waters?

He had a mental image, of the water levels ebbing and flowing, rising and falling, and imagined a turbine in a pit harnessing this energy. Then he thought of a sand sieve leading to each pit, through which sand would be filtered out of the water. A sieve too small for fish, so none would pass through and be affected.

Filled with confidence in his revelation, he filed for and got a patent.

A patent at the age of 14. Remarkable. Now follows the research, prototyping, testing, and development into a churning, flowing, masterpiece reaching millions.

The research came. But it showed him that tidal power had one key issue: low density.

To harness enough energy to make a real impact, Novek would need massive turbines. Even then, most of the world has tides too minor for sufficient energy generation.

Now comes the brainwave, doesn't it? The sudden spark in his mind which solves all these challenges.

Only it doesn't. Novek gave up, realising this idea was not practical.

But he did not give up on his dream of doing something to fight climate change. He just had to adapt and find better ideas. In his school lab, he thought he had come up with something: a cheap way to make Urea, a nitrogen-based fertilizer, one of the world's most common and widely used types. As he developed and researched, he kept coming across research papers with the name of a Yale University professor, Menachem Elimelech. Novek emailed him many times seeking advice, requesting access to advanced equipment, and trying to set up an in-person meeting, but he got no response. Finally, after he won several prizes at the 2015 ISEF, Novek sent Elimelech a long email with all the new things he had developed in the year he'd spent in his lab. This time, Elimelech replied with a one-line response asking Novek to meet in person.

It changed everything. Elimelech liked Novek's ideas and invited the 16-year-old to join his lab. The Yale professor recruited other researchers to help Novek. The result of their work was a peer-reviewed study published in the journal Environmental Science & Technology Letters in July last year. If everything were to work as planned, Novek's technology could capture carbon dioxide at $10 or so per metric ton, about 85% less than the industry standard.

While experts were reviewing the paper, Novek was busy applying to take part in the Carbon X-Prize, a competition aimed at finding the most effective carbon-capture technology with prizes worth $20 million to be given.

Novek's application made the cut, one of 22 teams to become an X-Prize semi-finalist. Now, Novek would have to show his technology worked outside of the lab. As part of the next round of the Carbon X-Prize competition, he had 12 months to build a pilot plant that could capture 200 kg of carbon dioxide per day from the exhaust gases of a power plant.

After pulling out of the X-Prize, Novek has doubled down on his tech. He's secured funding from an investor to build another pilot plant that will use actual waste gas from a power plant or chemical factory, and capture 1,000 kg of carbon emissions per day. (Novek wouldn't say who the investor is because of a confidentiality agreement.) He's also currently applying for a $3 million grant from the US energy department.

So Novek started with waves and sand, went on to urea and fertilisers, and ended with carbon capture. What a journey, which just shows that having the perfect answer isn't half as important as asking the right questions and challenging oneself on finding the answers and persisting in the face of challenges.

YOUR GUIDE TO SAVING THE WORLD

Milan and Ethan are role models, examples of teens who challenged the status quo to achieve greatness, completely remodelling the way electricity is generated in today's world and their communities. Not all of us need to be inventors (although perhaps some of us will make a big difference like them), but everyone can play a role in the shift towards a more environmentally friendly and clean tomorrow.

Of course, there is a lot of overlap between what you can do for this SDG and what you can do for Climate Action since both have the fundamentally same aim-

fighting climate change.

But apart from all the "using less" that the climate action chapter says we must do, there are other steps we can take for clean energy.

There are organisations like Student Energy that help thousands of students by supporting the development of clean energy. They're just a click away at https://studentenergy.org.

They have a Chapters program, which consists of student-led, post-secondary clubs spanning six continents that take action on energy in their communities. By joining or starting a chapter, you'll receive support from mentors at Student Energy and collaborate with a global network of young people.

They also give mentoring on clean energy and funding for projects around it. Learning more about this organisation and others like it could help you become a part, just like Milan and Ethan, of the war against fossil fuels. We can try to reduce our usage of fossil fuels in the short term, but we will be forever reliant on them if we do not find and understand clean energy sources as alternatives. We as teens can help with our drive to work towards this by joining organisations like Student Energy or coming up with ideas.

Jack Kemp

"Economic growth doesn't mean anything if it leaves people out."

Chapter 9

GROWTH GENERATORS

This SDG is perhaps the one that feels most distant, the furthest beyond our reach as teenagers. Among its objectives is "Sustained...economic growth, full and productive employment, and decent work for all."

We don't work in jobs, and many of us haven't even started studying Economics in school. As teens with many years to go for employment and contribution to the economy, it seems strange for us to concern ourselves with doing too much for this SDG.

But, as I have understood it, the economy works not on some deep college degree-level phenomenon- just people being able to produce and provide goods and services for others.

As early as grade 6, I saw this principle in practice, when at a school fair, I sold several copies of my book to parents and students. My dad, who studied Economics in college, and who leads businesses in the corporate world, told me that was what creating economic value was all about- create something that will be of value for others by meeting their needs, and there will be demand for it.

We can all contribute to the economy, just by creating products and services that are useful to others and make employment, also earning money to help support our families and fund our work and research. This is again tied with the innovation SDG, coming up with useful ideas that can stimulate economic growth by being interesting and useful to others. This is especially possible in a digital world where creating something of value doesn't require large machines or huge factories, but can often be accomplished by a kid in front of a computer, trying to solve an issue or make something others will want to use.

There are some teen heroes who have become members of the economy, making a difference and fuelling it with jobs, services, and money with their initiatives and brands.

***

TEEN HEROES WHO ARE SAVING THE WORLD

January 2014. A four-storey apartment building in Santa Clara, spread out over a wide area, with others like it stretching into the distance, all cloaked in a sprawl of greenery, trees shining bright green in the sun and rolling hills in the distance, beyond it all.

Inside, Shubham Banerjee, a 12-year-old wearing glasses and an orange hoody on a grey t-shirt, is in an elevator. He is looking at the floor numbers and sees under each of them a braille counterpart- a collection of raised dots.

Something lights up in his mind. Characteristically, he had been trying to come up with an engineering project, and here was something he had not considered yet- technology for the visually impaired. He did some research. He found that in the 1950s, 50% of visually impaired Americans had access to Braille materials. That had decreased to 10%. Why?

Text-to-voice software on phones and devices had replaced Braille as the main assistive tech for the blind. This might sound more convenient to us, but high-end smartphones are not accessible to everyone.

The fix would be to make Braille cost-effective. With Braille printers declining and fading away, someone was going to have to make a good case for their continued usage, and low cost would be a good argument to use.

The rate for a traditional Braille printer-embosser is $2,000. What if he could reduce it to $200?

So he set to work. He assembled all the materials in his home and from stores to find something that would be cheap and practical. His kitchen became a lab, pieces of Lego and electrical wires and batteries strewn out all over the place, with him furiously at work fusing together different components for hours on end. Often, he would be up till two in the morning working, with his father, Niloy, a software engineer, right at his side, giving him advice at each step and guiding him.

He made one attempt at making the printer. It failed. The materials simply weren't holding together well enough to get it to work. He tried again. Failed again.

Overall, there were six failed attempts, with some problem with his work emerging no matter what Banerjee did. Finally, he found something that worked.

His parents were very supportive and willing to encourage his effort, so they got him a $350 Mindstorms kit. Suddenly, his experiments became more like the steps in a manufacturing process, a process of creation of a product he could visualise very clearly.

Using Lego and some small electrical components, he made a printer. It was small, and rounded, firing bits of raised dots to imprint Braille.

He tested it.

On a metal plate, it printed the six dots of the Braille sequence- alphabet, in a way.

What would he do now? Sell it somewhere or give it to some company to use? Too easy. Too unambitious. Banerjee wanted the recognition and impact that his invention deserved.

He founded a company- Braigo Labs- to develop the printer for educational and home use. The company also gave instructions and guidance to anyone who wanted to try making replicas of Banerjee's creation.

"Braigo" was a name that arose very simply- a combination of "Braille" and "Lego", as simply as the product itself and its development and rise.

His work came in the local newspaper, the whole town abuzz with the news of a 12-year-old taking a stand and resurrecting an anachronistic, dying technology.

His story was thus heard by a young man in his mid-20s checking the Atlanta Times news as he sat down just before Breakfast, told by a mechanical, female voice droning on in synthetic, robotic tones. He was using a text-to-voice app, and the mere idea of a 12-year-old understanding the suffering of people like him and finding solutions impressed the man.

He was Henry Wedler, an acclaimed organic chemist who did his work without sight. A man who had been honoured by Barack Obama as a Champion of Change for a chemistry camp he set up for visually impaired students.

He reached out to Banerjee, who, with his father, took it to the University of California, where Wedler worked, to demonstrate.

News of his work spread, and soon, he could call himself a true entrepreneur- the founder of Braigo.

On February 21, CNN interviewed him. On February 22, two interviews with him were aired on the radio, by NPR and CBC. On February 29, NBC aired a program completely dedicated to Banerjee's story. The media was going crazy.

He got 13 awards and recognitions in 2014, and four the next year, everything from Best of America to a piece in a UNICEF publication

"Some [people] said that the market is not that big, or [that this is] a speciality product," Banerjee says, unfazed.

"I just went ahead with what I thought was right."

The young inventor will be participating in the Smithsonian's Innovation Festival at the National Museum of American History on September 26 and 27 in 2023. The two-day festival, a collaboration between the Smithsonian Institution and the U.S. Patent and Trademark Office, will look at how today's inventors—independent, and from companies, universities and government agencies—are shaping the future.

A low-cost Braille printer could be a game-changer for the blind, as physical aids, software and Braille materials can be expensive, and rehabilitation funding offered by the state is often only available for blind people who can show that they are working in specific jobs. "That's a narrow slice of the population, even more so in the blind community," he adds. "So for everybody else who can't qualify for state aid, any technology costs come out of pocket."

***

In Atlanta, Georgia, Maya Penn, an 8-year-old girl with curly hair spreading out like the whorls of a flower far wider than her head, in a green and black scarf draped around her neck and a black t-shirt, is walking down a paved sidewalk beside a clothing store. She looks in and points at a dress. "I want to make sustainable fashion. I want to build a collection."

Her mom looked at her like she never had before, wondering what had sparked this, before replying, "Figure out how to do that and what you need to accomplish that goal."

The next day, she went back to her home and pulled out old clothes from the drawers. She modified them, creating dozens of colourful headbands and scarves. It looked a lot like just another arty eight-year-old playing around with things. But the extent of her ambition was revealed two years later when she taught herself HTML. As she went on, her research told her about the environmental hazards of fashion- its materials and the way it is disposed of. This motivated her to push on and focus on sustainability in her work instead of just manufacturing the usual clothes.

In the next few months, she used this new skill to build a website selling her goods. The website was the first step in founding Maya's Ideas, a sustainable fashion brand. It expanded and drew many customers. It got featured in Forbes Magazine. Over the next three years, she gave three TED Talks on sustainability, and one of them went viral, with 2 million views.

She has several employees and operates through stores around the world.

This endeavour also branched off into many other efforts to make a difference, including an NGO called Maya's Ideas 4 The Planet, in which she designed and shipped eco-friendly sanitary pads to women in Haiti, Senegal, Somalia, and Cameroon. She was commended by President Obama for her efforts in tackling issues she was passionate about, and is sometimes taken aback at the great things her vision of a fashion collection had led to.

"Every endeavour and project I take on is both creative,

and makes a positive impact for the world. My innovation comes from that intersection of art and social good", she said in a September 2020 interview for Leading Ladies Africa.

YOUR GUIDE TO SAVING THE WORLD

In an age when all of us are consuming tonnes of things every day, in everything we do- from devices to apps to physical products- a simple way to contribute to the economy and create something of worth is just that- creating something, instead of limiting yourself to consuming media.

I love writing, which is why most of what I create and spread to others comes in the form of books. Everyone has their passions, hobbies, talents, and interests. Some of you may like singing. Others may be good at painting or drawing. You could start a blog. Not everything has to begin as a full-fledged business, with all the plans coming fully made from your head in the beginning. It all starts with a thought, with a hobby, from Maya's clothes to Banerjee's experiments. You could share your work on Instagram or any other medium that suits you, and let it grow from there, as you reach more and more people and gain even more drive to continue. There is an ex-student in my school, for instance, who passed out last year and took a year-long break before college to pursue singing and music, core passions for her which she is also studying at Berkeley. She released her first album and reached many thousands of listeners, kickstarting her career. Eventually, if you begin with the right direction and choice of activity, you will succeed and may be able to take it to a level where it is monetised.

Also, getting some experience of the real world, outside the insulated one of school, may help to understand how you can become part of it by doing something of your own that catalyses economic growth. I, for instance, have tried to do this through engagements in service initiatives, such as collaborating with Save the Children India or UNICEF. Economic impact or really any kind of impact is made in the bigger ecosystem, the bigger universe outside our cocooned lives, and exploring those areas is important. We may be teens, and we may be years away from being considered adults, but when it comes to stimulating economic growth, by finding solutions to problems, or creating businesses and ideas, in today's world, we can step up and take charge as heroes like Shubham and Maya show us.

Steve Jobs

"Innovation is the ability to see change as an opportunity, not a threat."

Chapter 10

INNOVATION ICONS

This chapter's title may seem imposing. "Industry, innovation, and infrastructure".

They sound like the heavy machinery of factories; the dignified, formal voices of company executives discussing in a meeting room; a grandiose speech of the prime minister; the cacophony of construction- the rolling of metal wheels, the breaking of boulders.

But it need not.

In today's age, companies and governments aren't the only ones responsible for creating new things, an age in which every one of us can learn skills that enable us to make new products that reach and benefit people.

I started learning coding in 2019. My parents told me it would help me create new apps and websites and would teach me an invaluable skill for the 21st century and my life.

I started by making test applications that just gave me practice on the most basic of code and functionalities, which could do little more than display random colours and messages.

But as I progressed into more advanced programming languages and software, I discovered the true power of coding and the joy of using it.

It started very early on- from making objects move on an animated interface and setting up static screens to creating chatbots, databases, games, and AI image recognition and object-detection applications.

Beyond the projects and assignments in the class's curriculum, I realised coding gave me the ability to bring original ideas of my own to life.

For instance, in 2019 I created an anti-bullying website, with material on the issue and how to deal with it, and it got a few hundred visitors every month for some time. Then, just a few months ago, I developed CricData, a database of all Indian T20I cricketers, with their statistics and head-to-head comparisons, which could be filtered to rank them or view visualisations of the data. It was a way of engaging with something I love, the sport of Cricket, but using technology to create a new way of enjoying it, and helping other kids enjoy it.

Innovation is a very broad and inclusive concept, much more so than we usually imagine. It is simply the act of using new ideas and methods, ideally to solve problems and help others.

TEEN HEROES WHO ARE SAVING THE WORLD

Dharavi. The word which, for the whole of India and the world, symbolises hardship and suffering.

Millions of people- men, families, women, children, the elderly, crammed into claustrophobic spaces between alleys and in tiny houses. In every square meter- think, a square with 1m sides- three people live. This is one of the most densely populated places in the world, and that is just the tip of the iceberg.

Your feet sink into open sewers, uncovered drainage channels festering with waste. The air is heavy, thick with contamination, and myriad particles infected with goodness knows what disease enters in through your nose and mouth. Your head spins and your sight blurs with the fatigue of dehydration and hunger.

This is the reality faced by over a million residents of Mumbai every day, and it feels especially ironic and cruel to see towering highrise buildings looming just a few hundred feet from the furthest houses in the slum.

In 2016, this is the reality faced by Ansuja Madiwal, 15, and many of her friends.

The Dharavi Diary Project is an initiative by filmmaker Navneet Ranjan, teaching girls how to code so they can develop apps addressing the slum's issues. "These kids didn't have dreams and aspirations because they live in such difficult circumstances", she says.

Indeed, for them, getting through the next day alive, without starving or going thirsty or catching diseases, was more than enough.

Until Ranjan and her team taught Ansuja and the others "how technology can be used to challenge the status quo".

Dozens of girls flocked to the building where the classes were happening, clustering themselves around each laptop. Some would hold papers on which they jotted down quickly brainstormed ideas, while a few would have laptops and be scrolling through them or typing and moving something with the cursor. Others would crowd on the sides and raise their voices in a chorus of repudiation and support and advice.

"When we joined the program we decided first to look at the problems that our neighbourhood and community faced, and then build apps to address them," Madiwal told The Hindu.

Using the MIT App Inventor, they created Women Fight Back, an application as powerful as its name, with an in-built alarm system that female users can set off if they are feeling uncomfortable- if they are being assaulted or harassed. It also contains many emergency contact numbers for the women to call and get aid quickly. This app was revolutionary for a place like Dharavi, where women would suffer in silence, and their suffering would be taken by many to be a part of life in the slum. Now, they would not need to cow down and be dominated, armed with weapons to rally others around them, and protect them.

Another issue was a lack of access to clean water. The slum often went without clean drinking water for days, and the open, filthy sewers also denied people water for other everyday uses.

The girls had the most reason to care about this issue because they frequently had to miss school on their hours-long trips to collect water from outside Dharavi.

So they made an app called Paani, which sets up online queues for water collection to systematise the process of collecting the most essential of all commodities for the slum, preventing crowds from fighting, avoiding delays and ensuring that everyone got their fair share.

In making these two apps, and many others, these girls have innovated.

They found solutions to very fundamental problems afflicting their lives and the lives of other members of their community, all through the drive and determination to stretch themselves and learn new skills, skills they would have barely heard of before and had no exposure to before the project.

***

All of us know that kids are excluded. All of us know it happens in our schools, in our classes, and among our friends. Many of us may have been excluded at some point, the kid who is bullied; the kid no one wants to talk to or show the others that they are talking to; the kid who has to sit alone at lunch, and walks around awkwardly searching for a welcoming face, or simply hunches down over their lunch at some isolated spot.

Natalie Hampton, in Sherman Oaks, California, is an 11th-grade student. "At my old school, I was completely ostracized by all of my classmates, and so I had to eat lunch alone every day. When you walk into the lunchroom and you see all the tables of everyone sitting there and you know that going up to them would only end in rejection, you feel extremely alone and extremely isolated, and your stomach drops."

When she joined her new school, she adjusted better and had several friends, but she felt strangely guilty about the plight of the kids who were excluded there too. She could empathise with them more than anyone else and felt like she had to help them.

"I wanted to create something that would address bullying, but in a positive way." After all, there is a limit to how much blunt force can achieve when complex social intricacies are involved, and cliques are at work.

So she made an app. An app? For an everyday problem that focused on people and the physical act of sitting? That sounds fantastic, like the dream of some tech-obsessed child insulated from the realities around her.

But perhaps it can work. Natalie proved that.

She named it "Sit With Us", a "lunch-planning app" where kids can find lunch tables if they don't know where to go. Kids can sign up as ambassadors for the "Sit With Us club", the group of kids using and supporting the use of the app, and let others know that they have "open lunches" – anyone who has the app can go sit there.

Some may say that an alternative solution would be better- just being more compassionate and kind in everyday life and encouraging that in schools. But how many kids actually have the courage and empathy to go up to someone who is "ostracised" and ask them to sit with them? Also, the mere act of asking to sit with someone you don't know feels "like you're labelling yourself as an outcast", Natalie says.

The app has succeeded in making a real change at her school. A couple of weeks after its launch, people were already posting open lunches and inviting the excluded kids to sit with them. New friends are being made, and a sense of belonging and companionship cultivated, all by the simple idea of one teen rising above the petty politics of her class with a smart and innovative solution.

YOUR GUIDE TO SAVING THE WORLD

All of us need to be part of the digital age and the breathtakingly fast rise of STEM and skills like coding in the 21st century. The Computer Technology Industry Association predicts a growth in tech jobs 2x the employment growth in other industries over the next decade. That is one of the reasons I take coding as more than just a temporary hobby but a field to be studied further and pursued in the years to come.

Coding and Artificial Intelligence will shape more and more processes in society as we grow older. Currently, these are fairly young technologies, with potential that is still being explored, making them perfect for shaking up the system of our world and creating change. Thus, learning some of these skills and applying them to solve issues, like the girls at Dharavi or Natalie, can truly help you become someone part of the quest to save the world and accomplish the SDGs.

STEM subjects are also increasingly gaining traction, as humankind develops further on these fronts- Science, Technology, Economics, and Mathematics. If at times you find Science boring and overwhelming or think things like Maths and IT to be dry, know that you can make really amazing things with this knowledge- Science tells us how the world works, and Maths teaches us analytical thinking and logic, which is very useful in coding.

No matter how fun you think they are the way you are taught them, realise that in themselves these subjects have the potential to broaden the scope of your impact on the world and ignite the spark of desire in us, the desire to be one of the changemakers of tomorrow, blazing away all the darkness and lighting a torch of progress and hope in this world.

So when WB Yeats said "Education is not the filling of a pail, but the lighting of a fire", he wasn't just using fancy metaphors and vocabulary to support teachers and schools. He was speaking about a truth, a truth which if more of us learn to understand and apply in our lives, we can emulate icons like Ansuja and her friends and Natalie and become part of innovation, industry, and infrastructure, the building blocks for a better tomorrow.

Pope Francis

"Inequality is the root of social evil."

Chapter 11

EQUALITY ENTHUSIASTS

We often hear of the unequal distribution of wealth and resources in the world. I figured that, of course, some people would be richer than others. That's the way the world is, isn't it? When I first saw the statistics, a few years ago, on just how unequal our world is, I was shocked.

The richest 1% own 46% of the world's wealth. The bottom 55% own 1.3%.

The signs of this are everywhere, from the slums we visited in earlier chapters to construction sites and children on the street. Inequality is not just a statistic. It is all around us, if only we can open our eyes and see it.

What's the problem with this? Well, it's absurd, simply preposterous for so much of the human race to be languishing in hellish conditions of starvation, unemployment, ignorance, and disease, while a few individuals, often just due to a chance of birth, lounge in luxury, getting the very best the human race has ever been able to give.

There are even more variables coming in the way of equal opportunity- gender, race, and caste. This is another case of humankind arbitrarily dividing itself along meaningless lines, unthinkingly condemning millions to abysmal lives they did nothing to deserve.

In the US, the typical white family's net worth is eight times the average black family's. In February 2020, the black American unemployment rate was exactly twice that of the White rate of 3%.

Age-old social issues are behind these disparities, and it may seem like in trying to bridge these gaps we are battling the entirety of society with all its prejudices and idiosyncrasies shaped by powerful forces for centuries.

But this SDG is rather similar to No Poverty and Gender Inequality since this too is about extending a helping hand to those who have not got fair opportunities due to them, and teens have taken similarly courageous initiatives to fight against and break down the societal barriers we usually deem immutable.

TEEN HEROES WHO ARE SAVING THE WORLD

Gideon Buddenhagen was in ninth grade in Oakland, California. He would go to Google's office in the city for coding classes every week called Google Code Next, in a short, wide, rectangular building with black-tinged glass and "Google" in large white letters.

In the US, racial inequality extends to computers and technological literacy. A 1997 study by the North Carolina and Syracuse Universities found that black students entered university with fewer technological skills, a serious handicap in the digital age when so much is dependent on technology and mastery of the new-age inventions that will shape economies and societies this century.

Gideon himself is a biracial Jewish student, to whom these inequalities were more than just academic knowledge, being something he saw among friends and family. He had volunteered to teach a third-grade black student computer science, and one day something struck him. He was experiencing the joy of learning computers at Google's classes and was aware of the advantages it offered him. Surely other students of colour merited the same chance?

So one day he approached his mentor at Google and said he wanted to create a program to teach computer and leadership skills to middle school students of colour.

Over the next few months, he sat at meetings with Google employees, who were very interested in his initiative, which, if it worked, they could adopt it to expand their efforts to teach more students.

They came up with Leadership in Motion, which went beyond the nitty-gritty of coding and computer science, also giving invaluable lessons on leadership to empower these kids of colour, often seen as lesser due to their ethnicity, with the sense that they could become leaders tomorrow.

Gideon spent 2020 and 2021 growing Leadership in Motion, connecting to local NGOs and organising after-school programs. Bridge the Gap College Prep helped initially in California, as his plans matched their purpose perfectly.

In 2022, he won the Diller Teen Tikkun Olam Award, a program of the Helen Diller Family Foundation. Tikkun Olam is a Jewish principle translating to "repairing the world", so this award was a clear celebration of the change Gideon had catalysed in his community, repairing the broken system of disparity that denied black, Hispanic, and other students of colour the opportunities they needed.

In the same year, Google adopted his program in many states, implementing it in several of their computer-teaching centres and bringing Gideon's idea to life on a massive scale, benefiting thousands of children.

Now, after graduating from high school, Gideon has set his sight on uncharted terrain- the East Coast, where he went to Brown University in August. He will be working with Google to take his program further and tear down the walls of exclusion and racism in another part of the nation. Already, by September 2022 he had taken Leadership in Motion to New York City.

It seems like Gideon's initiative knows no bounds. He just felt strongly about something, but also was connected to the right organisation which supported him in implementing and scaling his ideas. That is why, as mentioned in another chapter too, forming connections outside school with such bodies can help make a huge difference.

***

Armaan Singh Ahluwalia was just another 12-year-old in Delhi, feeling pity for the children begging at the traffic signal.

One day, he was with his mother, seeing a child walk around cars, banging on the windows and putting forth his hands with pleading eyes when he felt a sudden pang of sadness and enterprise. "I want to open a school for the poor children."

His mother was supportive and gave him complete license to take this dream forward in any way that he wished.

He started the school on a floor of his house, reserving four rooms for the students, naming it *Apne*, "Ours", a simple name but one that seems to thrive with a sense of community and hope. Getting them to come wasn't tough, but getting them to stay and benefit from the experience was.

He kept them interested with a mix of academics, sports and debating, doing what he enjoyed and sharing what he knew with the children.

The number of students kept rising. From 5-6, he now gets 25 every weekend and now has kept three floors in his building for them.

"It feels like I get a fresh breeze of life when I'm in the company of these children," said Armaan in an interview with the Statesman.

As his mother saw his son's vision growing into something more, she left her job at a multinational company to support him.

"I have no regrets about leaving my job and helping Armaan to start this school. It has given us much more happiness and understanding of the purpose of our lives."

Apne thrives because Armaan empathises with fellow kids and knows what they want and need to gain access to a well-rounded education. He organises football tournaments and matches, athletic-training sessions and theatre rehearsals.

"I want all these students to become well-educated and become all-rounders, to improve their quality of life," he says.

Apne has become a sensation in the neighbourhood, with other families donating stationery, books, uniforms, and money. They also bring their kids for birthday celebrations with the children and other special occasions. Food is also commonly sent from houses in the neighbourhood to ensure that the kids at Apne get good nutrition. Apne is more than a school- it is a second home for the kids.

Armaan spends at least one hour every day running the school, sometimes up to three to four hours. It is not easy for a 15-year-old to run a school with only his mother for help. Schools are typically run by several dozens of people together for hundreds or thousands of students.

This hefty undertaking has cost Armaan some of his time for himself, watching TV or playing video games. But he does not regret this.

"I have sacrificed these pleasures to get ultimate satisfaction and happiness while being in the company of the children from slums, who too love me," he says.

In the beginning, his mother says the children had "lost

faith in themselves", with little to live for. Armaan and his efforts do more than provide education, they reinforce our faith in humanity, and in the powerful force for good that an individual can be.

YOUR GUIDE TO SAVING THE WORLD

Neither Gideon nor Armaan possessed anything unique which enabled them to score victories against the supervillain of inequality. Gideon learned to code, but so do many of us. Aman had a remarkably supportive mother, but the idea and resolve came from within.

One thing the two had in common was their willingness to look beyond their comfortable, sheltered cocoons and take a broader view of society and those who are a part of it. Armaan could have sat back in his car and occupied his mind with school or the latest video game, but he chose to look outside and see what other children were facing.

I think that this is the first step in lifting those with inferior opportunities or fortunes in society, in creating more equality. All of us are vaguely aware of problems like poverty or discrimination, but how many of us make an effort to learn more or understand them beyond statistics and hearsay?

One way of doing this is to volunteer at NGOs and take opportunities to interact with the less privileged and get a better perspective on their problems while having an impact. This can also be done in your communities, as Armaan did while founding his school, by asking around and investigating the issue in your neighbourhood, where making a difference will be the easiest.

Another aspect of fighting the villain of inequality is applying your skills and interests to help the underprivileged. Gideon has coding and computers; Aman used his passion for football and theatre to power his sessions with his students and expose them to various skills and ways of thinking.

Your interests and hobbies, whether in sports, academics, or anything else, need not stay private; you can share them with others, especially those who are otherwise usually denied access to the opportunities that gave you those skills, to introduce them to a more diverse range of activities and ideas.

In the darkness that the marginalised and impoverished are imprisoned in, even the smallest shaft of light can be world-changing. Just be concerned and willing to do something, willing to provide the heat to ignite that spark and the torch to shine upon their lives. Then perhaps they can get some of your light, and receive chances more equal to yours. As Eleanor Roosevelt said, "It is better to light one small candle than curse the darkness."

Henry David Thoreau

"What is the use of a house if you don't
have a decent planet to put it on?"

Chapter 12

SUSTAINABILITY SUPERSTARS

The building I live in, in the Mumbai suburb of Powai, is in front of the slopes of a forested hill. It stands under blue skies by day and starlit skies by night. From my window, far below, I see a thick canopy of trees over the ground, their boughs concealing the forms of the forest's creatures. Just beyond is a lake, crystal clear water shimmering in the sun and reflecting the dark green, gently rolling hills of beyond, which lead the eye into the horizon, where more such woods stand.

Sounds too good to be true, right?

It does. This is what my neighbourhood would indeed have looked like just a few decades ago, but development and urbanisation have led to several irreversible changes.

There are many trees, and there are hills, but the rapid development of the neighbourhood means that there is more. My apartment stands in front of two massive structures at least ten storeys high, roads filled with traffic and the noise and bustle of construction as more buildings come up. It stands under skies that are hazy by day due to all the pollution. From my window, I see a dozen buildings of concrete raised up, dwarfing the few trees scattered here and there. From my balcony, I can see Powai Lake, which once must have been azure blue, but now is stained green.

I don't mean to sound pessimistic. The area where I live is immeasurably more "green" than many other neighbourhoods in a city like Mumbai, but that in itself brings home the tragedy of what urbanisation does to our environment.

Researching for my book *Back from the Brink* taught me many lessons about how dire this issue is. 46% of endangered species live in cities, and hundreds of thousands of species are victims of this unfettered development and urban sprawl, which hurls emissions into the air, lays forests and plains waste, and infests water and soil with poison.

But there was another story I learned about. The story in which we triumph, in which urban communities unite to set right these wrongs, igniting a fire in the darkness as the light of thousands of individuals comes together to give warmth and sanctuary to the planet.

Everywhere, there are cities that have made themselves more sustainable, with the power of communities filled with a collective drive to defend the natural world from urbanisation's perils.

In Chicago, Lights Out Chicago, a movement to turn

off the lights at night to prevent birds from colliding and dying, saved 7.5 million birds in 26 years.

In Andhra Pradesh, 90 urban donors and tribals with nests saved the Great Hornbill from extinction, increasing populations by 25%.

In Vengurla, Maharashtra, literally 100% of households started segregating waste, protecting the nearby beaches from plastic, tripling turtle nesting sites and populations in a couple of years, starting the species' meteoric rise in the state.

And, often, the greatest of endeavours are started by one person, or a small group of people, feeling discontent with the status quo, but not stopping there, and stepping forward to make a difference.

TEEN HEROES WHO ARE SAVING THE WORLD

Not far from we started, near my home and the hills and the trees and the lake, lives a 13-year-old boy named Ayaan Shankta.

He would visit the lake with his parents. He saw the water move further away from his feet as he stood on the bank, and algae and shrubs mushrooming and smothering the water.

This is eutrophication, a sudden proliferation of algae caused perhaps by mineral-rich chemical waste from drains and fertilisers.

Eutrophication can demolish aquatic ecosystems. The algae suck in oxygen, suffocating the animals below. They block sunlight, as fish and underwater plants grow frail and wilt and die.

Sewage flowing into the lake has reduced levels of dissolved oxygen (DO) to the lowest since 1961. People living closest to it say that 30-40 dead fish wash ashore every day.

His parents would take him there for clean-ups, but as he plucked plastic bags from beds of algae, he knew he wasn't addressing the root of the problem. Surely he could do something about the algae?

He did. He started a project- Conservation and Rehabilitation of Powai Lake.

He began by conducting a detailed survey of it, noting down his observations about the conditions more thoroughly than even the experts had in their censuses.

He learned more about the hidden forces at work in polluting the lake. The lake had become a dumping ground for offices, hotels, houses, and construction sites. People were also pumping water for construction operations, unrestrained by any authority.

He wrote an action report on the lake's condition, outlining the issue and key steps that the government and the community needed to take. In a competition- the Homi Bhabha Balvaidnyanik Competition- it got a gold medal for its scientific rigour and firmness with which it created a roadmap for saving the lake.

He felt small in front of these hundreds of people callously killing off the ecosystem, his care seeming powerless before their thoughtlessness. So he sought allies.

He joined forces with several local NGOs, and with

them spread his voice far and wide across Powai, urging people to come and take an interest in what was happening to the "lake" in the "lake view" label given to their apartments.

He urged them to come and do something about the situation. He organised weekly clean-ups faster and more successfully than ever before, with droves of people coming and removing all waste from the waters. The community, at last, seemed to be doing something.

Meanwhile, having unleashed his inner leader, pioneer, and researcher he showed his prowess as an engineer and innovator.

He built a robot.

He designed the "Autonomous Spatial Pollution Detection Robot", a self-driving robot which swims across the lake, detecting pollution and eutrophication.

Everywhere around the world, conservation organisations, especially youth-oriented ones, were abuzz with the news of this young boy acting on a colossal ecological mess no one else wanted to dirty their hands in.

AFN (Action for Nature) named him as one of 25 International Young Eco-Heroes and said his project was the third most "heroic" in the world.

What do heroes do? Do they do what they do for fame?

No. Real heroes step up to make a difference to others. They are on a mission that is bigger than them. As Ayaan says, "My mission is for the lake to regain its past glory as a clean and vibrant body of water."

True heroes aspire, inspire, lead, and work towards

restoring glory not to themselves but to the world around them, uplifting their entire communities with them.

That is what Ayaan did.

***

Hundreds of colours flash in the sky, snaking through the air, festooned on a large ship.

This is Tampa, Florida, and the Gasparilla Pirate Festival is happening. Crowds line the path in the Seddon Channel, looking on at this pirate ship as it pretends to attack the city, thrusting forth at the shores and firing mock cannonballs.

But the sky is then lit with brighter colours, a shower of green and yellow and purple and red. Hundreds of necklaces have just been thrown, hurling through the air and pelting upon the surface, vanishing into the depths below.

A spectacular display. Shining with more beauty and natural brilliance than most phenomena.

Correction: *plastic* brilliance.

These beads are made of a material that fixes its synthetic surface deep into the seabed. A material that tears into the bodies of fish from the inside, clogging their windpipes and arteries, making lacerated, stripped-down ghosts out of living beings.

A thirteen-year-old boy in a dark blue shirt stands on the quay. His eyes are empty, void of emotion, as they look upon the glorious display with their solid pupils blurring around the edges. He is on the brink of tears.

Five years later, an article appears on a page of the Washington Post. "He urges fest to end the tradition of dumping beads into waterways", the headline declares.

As we read on, we learn that the eponymous "he" is Demetri Sedita, who says that the tiny bits of plastic threatens the area's "Shorebirds, manatees, dolphins, stingrays, and common fish such as sheepshead."

To understand how this was possible, we have to go back to 2015.

That boy standing on the quay had been Demetri. In a few days, he, sitting at the dinner table, spoke to his brother Ethan, sitting across from him.

"I think we should do something about the beads."

Ethan agrees.

The two are in the bay the next day, slinging metal hooks in their right hands.

Below the water, the crescent shape of a hook moves in the shadows. It swings, slow and steady. There is a faint crackle as it whizzes at and tears through sand and pebbles, and the debris sprays in a dark splash.

In the darkness, it grips the lengthy, rope-like form of a green bead, shining aquamarine in the light, and like a tentacle, hoists it up.

In a few moments, the bead appears on the surface, floating benignly, steadily and slowly in the wind.

A few hours later, amidst the dark depths below, the surface of the ocean is broken by a streamlined form plunging in as bubbles foam in spirals.

It is Demetri, scuba diving under the waves, right into the mess others have created.

In the middle of the night, a small shape, whirring and beeping, hits the surface with a plop, leaving bubbles foaming and microscopic waves rippling as it disappears. It is Demetri's drone, the drone with which he once discovered a shipwreck from the American Civil War. Now, he records the beads with it.

He amasses a colossal database of recordings, unmasking the apocalypse below the waves, out of sight, out of mind, out of light, enveloping the seas in a night of death.

He and his brother approach their parents for help. Together, they collect an army of people, an army of Tampa Bay residents whom Demetri and Ethan woke up to the catastrophic impacts of their Gasparilla Festival revelry.

Demetri has grown the initiative from an internal fantasy to a lifted necklace, from a brotherly effort into a familial and communal war. Now, he grows it into a government project: The Bead-Free Bay Initiative, led by mayor Jane Castor and Demetri.

In August 2019, he grew it into a global sensation, christened "youth ambassador" by the organisation EarthEcho International.

But why did he start this? Not for fame or recognition, not for the hyperbolic praise of his fellow Tampa Bay dwellers or the conservation community. Not even for the wordless, unheard thanks of the fish he would save. He started Green Gasparilla to make a difference. Everything else is tangential.

Thus, he sighs when he says that "Most people continue to throw the beads."

Imagine yourself, content with those beads you didn't throw at the festival. Now imagine you are Demitri, dissatisfied with all his work, even with the lives he has saved and the slaughters stopped.

See and admire the vision, the undying ambition and conviction to make the world a better place, in the mind of a thirteen-year-old.

YOUR GUIDE TO SAVING THE WORLD

To make a difference in your communities, it is important to find something you are passionate about, a direction you want to help take your community in. But to really translate this into action, you must involve yourself in the lives of others and the others in your efforts.

Be aware of and attend community events that have an impact on issues.

Take advantage of any volunteering opportunities in your community, such as working for NGOs or other local initiatives.

Take the help and collaboration of your family and friends in anything you can do. Demitri is a prime example here, recruiting his brother and friends, and eventually enlisting the help of the Mayor.

This SDG is the least individualistic of them all at first sight, being about communities working together to achieve something, but community action is essential for nearly all SDGs. After all, humankind is one big ecosystem of smaller groups- cities, states, countries- and to really save the world, you must look at the problems not as abstract concepts you can deal with alone but as nuanced realities faced by real people around you, which you can only help deal with by taking the community along.

One of the downsides of our modern lifestyles is that we spend too much time in virtual worlds instead of engaging in the real world around us. However, that's not to say technology is bad. It all comes down to how you use it. Social media need not only be places you go to post photos of yourself and friends but can help exponentially broaden the definition of the word 'community', by connecting you with like-minded teens from other cities and even countries. Use that not just to make friends, but to engage on issues you feel strongly about, and to learn from each other.

Communities can be many things. They can be destroyers or saviours. They can be pollutants or cleansers. They can be killers or life-givers. What they truly become is up to you.

Spiderman

"With great power, comes great responsibility."

Chapter 13

ROLE MODELS OF RESPONSIBILITY

In my school, when it was announced that as a grade, we were doing a service project on Sustainable Fashion, I was disinterested, even sceptical. I had heard a lot about such a concept but had thought it to be yet another attempt by companies to make themselves part of the "Sustainability" narrative and act as if they are doing the world a great service while paying lip service to adopt eco-friendly materials and manufacturing.

The name, "ThriftShift", which to me felt like a forcedly witty usage of assonance to label a low-impact project, didn't help.

I couldn't be more wrong.

As I got involved in the project, researching for writing a School Newsletter article, I learned that of the clothes we wear, 85% are disposed of in landfills.

There, they rot away over time, spewing methane and greenhouse gases as they decompose. This also ejects toxic chemicals and dyes into soil and groundwater, the same soil we will entrust our crops, drinking water, and lives with.

The fashion industry is thus responsible for 10% of annual global CO_2 emissions.

But the worst part? 95% of this need never have reached the landfill. It could easily have been recycled or reused or donated to someone in need.

As a grade, we planned to collect old clothes before they were disposed of and wasted away in landfills, and modify and repurpose them so someone else could purchase them. Our teachers came up with an idea about using the money gained from this- we could donate the funds to the SOS Children's Village in Alibaug, an organisation that gives underprivileged children without parents a home, education, and opportunities for a better life.

We began with the collection. We placed large boxes on every floor of the school, near the elevator areas and staircases.

Every day, I would pass the collection boxes on my way through the corridors and would find them empty. I would find not a single garment kept inside, and few in the school community were interested in contributing to our cause.

But we did not give up.

I went to the teacher and told her I wanted to do something.

I made posters, which we put all around the school, and wrote articles for the School Newsletter.

Many of us went to the classes of other grades, younger and older, to inform them of this and encourage them to contribute.

In the end, we had amassed an assortment of dozens of myriad items, from t-shirts to dresses to jeans to shorts, for all ages and of all kinds. We amassed all of these in one large box in our classroom, satisfied with our work.

It was now that the practical, hands-on aspect of ThriftShift began.

For the next month, we worked on modifying these clothes. Many were worn out by years of use, so we patched them up and refined them to make them presentable. Several others were serviceable and with no serious defects, but we still used our creativity to improve and embellish them so they would sell better and give us more funds for the SOS village.

Some we bored into or sliced apart with scissors, reshaping t-shirts into crop tops or perfectly plain jeans into ripped ones. Some we embellished with ribbons and stars on their surface; on others, we applied paint or placed stickers, decorating them and giving them a new lease of life, a new aesthetic. Even I, never particularly keen on art and craft and with dubious artistic skills, tried modifying a couple of pieces, motivated by the knowledge that I was working for something worthy.

But from the collection experience, in which without our toil to encourage support, no one was coming near the boxes, we knew that our efforts would go waste if we didn't make it more mainstream in the school consciousness.

We tried to create a trailer using a skit, to engage and entertain while sharing the message.

We made several teaser videos to post on the school's social media account, one of which I created.

We sent out numerous emails to the entire school community, with the help of the principal and the student council

All of this focused on one date: October 19, 2022, the day of the Auction.

A lot of planning went into this. We decided to combine it with a major school function to gain access to the droves of parents who would be coming that day.

We prepared the set-up and planned the logistics and schedule, beginning with a speech that spoke about our journey and motives, followed by a silent auction of numerous items, in which bids were written on paper, and the main auction at the end. We set our prices at a level high enough to raise money and low enough to be attractive, optimising our collection.

It would take place at 5:00 PM. We stayed after school to be able to do it, and I remember sitting in the library at 4:00, trying to occupy myself with reading a book when what was really going through my mind was the speech I would have to give to the parents about the cause, galvanising them to part with some of their money for our cause.

At 5:00, things were not quite ready for my speech. People were still coming in, we were setting up the boards for the silent auction items labels, placing the hanger with the clothes in the right place, and doing mic-checks.

At 5:25, I began. I spoke about what I truly felt, about the weight of the issue, of the tons of greenhouse gases contaminating our atmosphere and the millions of clothes that go waste every day. Unthinkingly, unknowingly, and unhesitatingly, adding to our planet's woes. I also spoke of the children at the SOS village, denied even a family, let alone the material necessities of shelter and food and education.

"So a few clothes sold, a few thousand rupees made…. what sort of a difference is that? But as Jane Goodall once said, 'Every individual can make a difference every day by making conscious choices'."

The auction began with gusto as we encouraged the visiting parents to buy the repurposed clothes, some of us even modelling them on stage, or talking about the exotic design features. We had fun, but we also raised tens of thousands of Rupees.

On the 10th of November, we went to Alibaug for our school trip and met the schoolchildren and the people who ran the SOS Children's Village. The President thanked us for our contribution, which they would spend on purchasing infrastructure for the children and facilitating their education. We were then asked to teach the children some of our skills in modification, and even as I sat there, the green vista of Alibaug stretched out to the horizon, and as I compared that to the filth of a landfill, I felt whole for a few moments. At least I have been part of making some semblance of an impact in working towards such a reality and escaping the clutches of landfills.

We were just a bunch of teenagers, but together, using our combined talents, we made a small difference to a big issue.

TEEN HEROES WHO ARE SAVING THE WORLD

You are in Lagos, Nigeria. Mercifully, though, you are away from the jam-packed streets with honking cars and bustling markets, and litter-lined roadsides. You are in a green field, bordered by a perimeter of canvas and shade, in which there are white chairs in which is seated a crowd of hundreds of people, looking on at the teens in front of them with interest.

There is a tall boy in a black t-shirt and trousers right in front of you. Nearly his entire upper body is draped in red plastic spoons and fabric, giving the aesthetic of a thick trail of blood in the night. He is standing in a ring of boys and girls his age, some adorned in clumps of plastic bottles, others clothed in white dresses with splashes of colour from newspapers, made by sticking together and solidifying dozens of scraps of paper.

They are walking steadily in a circle, without stopping or speaking or causing any other interruption to the proceedings.

You go up to the boy and ask him what he's doing.

He turns out to be named Nethaniel Edegwa, aged 16. "We can see that we are all being affected by the climate change, so I really want to make a difference."

All those walking in the ring are more than just a random group of teenagers or even just models who like the clothing. They are environmental activists opposed to the plastic scourge that plagues our cities and populations.

They have all raised their voice against this material in the past, and are anxious to be able to do something to turn the tide against irresponsible and excessive consumption of this ecologically disastrous substance.

They have spent the past several months working with Greenfingers Wildlife Initiative to repurpose plastic and paper objects from cutlery to toys to bottles in a way that prevented them from going to waste but also intrigued, caught attention, and inspired others.

Today is Trashion Show, a day for raising awareness about environmental pollution and celebrating the tons of plastic those teens have saved our planet from. This is part of an initiative by Greenfingers Wildlife Initiative, an organisation out to "recycle as many plastics as possible".

But as you see those teenagers, some smiling, some looking vaguely uncomfortable or worn out under the hot Nigerian sun, prepared to dress up in slightly eccentric and absurd clothing in an age where we're all so concerned about our looks and what we wear, you cannot help but appreciate the fact that Greenfingers wouldn't achieve much without their commitment.

YOUR GUIDE TO SAVING THE WORLD

Responsible production and consumption may seem like a joke in an age of incessant manufacturing, industry, and advertising, when we are all consumers, fuelling the economy by taking more and more while the environment suffers. We have all heard this narrative before, somewhere or another- perhaps in school, an article, or a Ted Talk.

We all know about the menace of plastic, choking turtles in the seas, and have, without exception, been lectured on its evils numerous times.

The stories of ThriftShift and the Trashion Show are but mere episodes, anecdotes in the broader tale of waste and unscrupulous consumption. But, at the very least, there are a few things we can learn from them, one of them being that we can reduce our waste in many, often unexpected and innovative ways. And making clothes from plastic and reusing and modifying clothes is just the tip of the iceberg.

There are several steps we can all take to play our part in working towards the fulfilment of this SDG:

- 💡 Avoid using disposable goods: Use permanent mugs instead of paper cups that need to be thrown away every time. Replace non-reusable paper towels with reusable dishcloths.

- 💡 Use paper straws can be used instead of plastic ones which are thrown away and add to the piles of waste in the sea, imperiling turtles and marine life. Jute or cloth bags can be made use of instead of the plastic ones that have become the norm.

- 💡 Instead of throwing old and unused articles, donate them to charity: Several charities are looking for such materials to give to the needy. One, Goonj, sends its trucks to a place visible from my home for collecting people's old objects. Donating books and clothes here stop that waste from ending up in the landfill and adding to pollution and may also be useful for an underprivileged family.

- Think about innovative ways to reuse items in your home: In my home, newspapers are not just read- they are used in the kitchen to keep materials and food on them and protect the counters from getting dirty. Newspapers can also go into shoes to help them retain their shape. Microwave trays can become dishes or plates. Cans can store lunch. Reusing is not restricted to creating new uses for old items. It may also be about continuing to use old items in the same way without throwing them. Instead of getting rid of broken furniture and toys and buying new ones, have them repaired or fix them yourself.

- Segregate Waste: Use multiple bins at home instead of just one for all waste- one for wet waste, and another for dry. This prevents the waste from getting mixed up and eases their recycling and proper disposal. It is estimated that a family of 4 can reduce annual waste from 1000 tonnes to less than 100 through waste segregation.

I remember Jane Goodall's quote once more: "Every one of us can make a difference every day through conscious choices". Waste is all around us. It is what we make with nearly everything we do every single day. It is up to us to adopt more sustainable and responsible lifestyles for the good of the planet.

Speaking of saving the planet, let's rise high above the dirt and soil and go to the heavens, where greenhouse gases are heating our Earth and threatening our future.

Barack Obama

"We are the first generation to feel the impact of climate change and the last generation that can do something about it."

Chapter 14

CLIMATE CHANGEMAKERS

In 2014, I went on a holiday to Venice. A beautiful city of cobbled streets and bridges above crystal clear waters, the narrow forms of gondolas gently gliding across their surfaces.

In June 2022, I visited the Maldives for five days. I would see from my room vibrant, clear, aquamarine seawater stretched out to the horizon, the streaks of the stripes on fishes and the fins of sharks and the discs of rays moving just below. Under the sea was another world, governed by different laws and ruled by different beings, but it felt so close.

These paradises, so close to nature, symbolised a certain permanence, as they were built on foundations so primaeval and ancient.

Until I learned they could disappear in the blink of an eye, beneath the crest of a massive wave. Studies show that 80% of the Maldives could become uninhabitable by 2050, and it and Venice could be completely submerged by 2100.

All thanks to climate change, rising temperatures expanding water and melting ice, thus swelling our oceans and raising sea levels.

Climate change does not just affect those close to the natural systems it corrupts- its impacts will be felt much closer to home.

By 2050, McKinsey India estimates a 25% increase in flash flood intensity and a half-metre rise in sea level, negatively impacting 2-3 million people.

I had a friend who moved here from Jakarta, a city whose fortunes are- quite literally- sinking. Unsustainable groundwater pumping and depletion are sinking it, making it a sitting duck for rising sea levels. The Indonesian government, panicking, plans to move the capital city 100 miles, taking 10 years and costing $33 billion.

The climate crisis can feel overwhelming at times. An analysis by the University of Graz says that it could kill up to 3 billion people by 2200.

"Eco-anxiety" is the term for the panic and fatalism that such statistics, that the vision of our Earth, sacred and core to our being, being ravaged and destroyed, can bring.

That is why many teens who are environmentally aware face "eco-anxiety", and are plunged into depths of depression and stress about the condition of our planet.

Sometimes, I have to stop worrying too much about it and try to adopt a more positive, solution-oriented mindset.

We must not bow down before this menace. Remember, it is one we have created ourselves, and only we can vanquish it.

TEEN HEROES WHO ARE SAVING THE WORLD

Everywhere, teens are living in fractured realities, homes torn apart and destabilised by warming and fires and floods.

Castlemaine is a small town in Victoria, Australia, with a population of 7,500. A town that, during the Gold Rush of the 20th century, was home to the richest goldfield, where settlers would flock in the thousands.

It lies towards the north-west of a state, in the heart of a semi-arid climatic region, but in case that appears to betray a lack of biodiversity, do not be deceived- in these conditions thrive gold-yellow grass standing in endless plains, dotted with woodlands and bushlands.

When the scorching sun heats the grass to the ignition point, it catches ablaze, and wildfires start.

Milou Albrecht, 15, would have heard of the fires raging a few miles away, and seen spires of smoke rise into the sky. She knew of the imminent danger of these disasters reaching her hometown, and founded School Strike for Climate Change Australia, made up of hundreds of adamant schoolchildren prepared to strike and do anything for the protection of their bushland and their city. The German corporation Siemens had been running a mining project that threw out tons of carbon dioxide into the atmosphere, imperilling the local climate.

Albrecht's group joined an army of organisations battling the mines. A petition against it got 60,000 signatures, and School Strike for Climate Change itself has pressured Siemens to call off the project. Under mounting pressure, Siemens has said it is considering quitting it.

***

Louisiana has a humid, subtropical climate, nourishing forests, marshlands, and black mangroves.

Jayden Foytlin, 16, saw this beloved world of nature and trees and water coexisting and mingling with leaves and roots, disappearing under the waves.

Louisiana has been tormented by violent storms and flash flood emergencies as the climate warms, especially dangerous for such an already humid climate and water-filled ecosystems.

Something drastic had to be done, which drew attention and alarm and anger.

Foytlin joined 20 other young activists from across the nation in an initiative to sue the Federal Government for its irresponsible environmental policies.

The lawsuit says the federal government has knowingly caused the Earth and the country to slide further into the mess of climate change, encouraging the production of oil, gas and other fossil fuels, causing the planet to warm and infringing on several of the plaintiffs' fundamental rights when it has known that the Earth was warming since 1965.

The Supreme Court responded by saying "the breadth of the respondent's claims is striking" and not acting.

Hell, yes. But not more striking than the reality of drowned cities, burning forests, and storm-wrecked homes millions are seeing.

While this action may not have led to change, Foytlin's courage of conviction is inspiring, and also an example that we should not be led only by thoughts of whether we will succeed or fail, but by whether the cause we are fighting for is worth it. And what is more worth it than the preservation of our world?

***

We have all heard of Greta Thunberg, a Swedish climate activist who has rocked the world with her speeches and ceaseless campaigning.

Sweden is an idyllic Scandinavian country of fjords and fields and ravines and cold seas, responsible for just 0.45% of the world's emissions. Surely other countries more globally relevant to climate change need someone like Greta?

We often forget that such teens are more widely dispersed than we think.

India has its own Greta Thunberg- Ridhima Pandey.

She is from Uttarakhand. The Northern State (which is what its name means) is famed for its beauty; towering mountains, valleys of fragrant flowers and meadows and green hills. Climate change has shaken the foundations of Uttarakhand's stability, throwing up the worst of the elements in unforeseen ways.

Tectonic plates in the mountains have wreaked havoc in landslides, burying hundreds of people beneath them and causing roads and towns to crumble. Floods have wreaked havoc on many parts of the state, killing 1,000 people in 2013. 100,000 people had to be evacuated.

Ridhima was born in 2008 in a world where climate change was tearing apart the very fabric that held her community and state together.

From the very beginning, acting to mitigate climate change was hardly an option. How soon would she be one of those having to migrate elsewhere in the country, leaving behind all she held dear?

At the age of nine, she filed a suit against the Indian government for not taking enough steps to combat climate change. This was dismissed, but it was a sign of things to come.

In 2019, she was applying for a Norwegian visa for a trip to Oslo. Somewhere, in the office, perhaps in a conversation about the climate activists in the region or the upcoming summit, perhaps said with a vaguely cynical and flippant tone, she heard of an organisation of young climate activists.

She approached it immediately and was selected alongside a few others to go to New York for the 2019 UN Climate Action Summit.

On 23 September 2019, she was rewarded, at the age of 11, with the opportunity to speak to dozens of world leaders about their failure to manage global warming.

With 15 children, including Greta Thunberg, she filed a complaint, not to the UNEP (United Nations Environmental Program) or the UN as a whole, but to the United Nations Committee on the Rights of the Child. After all, they were children, and while they could not speak the most authoritatively on big things, they could attest to how climate change was jeopardising their existence and livelihood- violating some of their most basic rights.

They accused five countries of violating the Convention on the Rights of the Child due to their abject failure in addressing the climate crisis.

She joined Thunberg and 13 others again when they sent a legal petition to António Guterres, Secretary-General of the UN, to declare the climate crisis a global level 3 emergency.

Earlier the same month, she had led a climate strike for the activist group FridaysForFuture in Dehradun and, with Ella Marie Haetta Isaksen, spoke at the Xynteo Exchange on global warming. She was now firmly part of the global activist network- this had become the primary purpose of her life.

She returned to India and appealed to Prime Minister Narendra Modi in December to abort a plan that would ravage Mumbai's Aarey Forest for a Mumbai Metro project, amplifying the cries of the crowds of protesters. This was probably the most concrete demonstration of the change she could bring- in a few months, the government had shifted operations elsewhere, leaving the forest, one of the last large wild ones in Mumbai, standing.

She also dared to speak about an often-neglected issue in political circles- the Ganga River. The problem of the plastic and filthy waste strewn in the stream is supposed to have been taken care of by now- the government launched the Ganga Action Plan in 1985. But it has not. An inconvenient truth, discussing which is counterproductive for politicians, and Pandey rightly pointed out that they claim to clean the river while it is just as contaminated as 30 years ago.

With her whole life ahead, the very thought of all the things she can do and the minds she will change is amazing.

YOUR GUIDE TO SAVING THE WORLD

Climate action, as the above examples may have shown, is a very personal problem. Every part of our lifestyles is responsible for adding to our ecological impact, and making small changes can thus fight climate change:

- Do not overuse electronic devices and plugs. A California University study found that 25% of all energy is spent on devices, so reducing your screen time, apart from being good for the eyes and finding constructive hobbies, also reduces emissions.

- Reducing meat consumption- the meat industry is behind 25% of Greenhouse Gas emissions due to the methane released by grazers and emissions from transport etc. You could adopt a more plant-based diet, such as a reducetarian (half-vegetarian) or not eating meat on certain days of the week.

- Cut down on the use of plastic- reuse and adopt alternatives such as reusable straws and bags. After reaching landfills and burning, plastic leaves a massive carbon footprint- 393 times that of a tote bag, even when reused. Commitment to removing this material from our lives is essential, for climate change as much as for responsible production and consumption.

Back to Ridhima. At age 13, she already has a biography: *Children vs Climate Change*. In it, she sums up her quest in two sentences:

"I want to save our future. I want to save the future of all the children and all people of future generations".

That future she refers to is our collective future- the future we teens will inherit. I hope more of us can have the grit of heroes like Ridhima to not just be anxious about the problem of Climate Change but act on it.

Arthur C. Clarke

"How inappropriate to call this planet Earth, when it is quite clearly Ocean."

Chapter 15

UNDERWATER UPLIFTERS

When I first moved to Mumbai in 2014, I soon learned that there was a beach near my school- Juhu Beach. Once, when my parents and I were in that area, I asked them if we could go to the beach someday.

"It's filthy", my mother said.

"How?", I asked. The only beaches I had seen before were on holidays, and those had been clean and beautiful.

I got the answer when I went there on a school trip in Grade 3, in 2017. I saw plastic bags, packets of chocolate, and plastic bottle caps, strewn out across the beach, not a single patch of sunlit, resplendent sand to be seen. The teachers asked us to help in a clean-up, and I remember dragging a bottle from beneath the sand and wondering why more people didn't come to clean this place.

In 2018, the next year, a guest speaker came to our

school- Afroz Shah, the man who had succeeded in transforming Versova Beach from a garbage dump into a thriving ecosystem.

He spoke to us of how he had been angered by the mess on the beach his apartment overlooked, starting with plucking plastic bags from it by hand with his 84-year-old neighbour. For 6-8 weeks they worked like this, in a pair, continuing even when they scarcely observed a single dent in the piles of plastic.

That was until they got support. By the end of the first year, dozens of volunteers had joined them, picking up 50,000 kilograms of waste from everywhere on the beach. The United Nations Environment Programme called it the "world's largest beach clean-up in history". The government supplied them with a machine to remove plastic, and the UN helped as well. By 2018, 5 million kgs of plastic were gone, and the turtles and dolphins were slowly returning, hatching eggs on the sand and swimming in the waters offshore.

This was my introduction to the concept of a beach clean-up, and, my word, was it a powerful one. While writing my book *Back from the Brink,* I learned more about the ecological importance of beach clean-ups, which have more value than just making beaches look better or even helping the animals on the beach or immediately offshore.

After the plastic is disposed of, it either ends up in a landfill or runs down streams, rivers, drains, and waterways to the ocean. But not straight to the ocean- first, they deposit on the beach.

In short, the plastic that is on the beach will be the plastic that will eventually land in the ocean, and we all know what happens after that.

Luckily, beach clean-ups are a solution, but they require effort en masse and commitment from those who start the movements and support them.

Here's a story of how two teenage girls from Bali completely reversed the situation with a simple desire to act and save the famous beauty of their island home.

TEEN HEROES WHO ARE SAVING THE WORLD

Two sisters, Melati and Isabel Wijsen, aged 13 and 11 in 2013, had a class in school about influential leaders- Nelson Mandela, Martin Luther King Jr., and Mahatma Gandhi. They didn't leave it dismissing it as another cliched lecture on the greatness of famous people- they went away wanting to be like Gandhi.

It sounds like a fantastical and vague dream, especially for two young children, but they were serious.

"My sister and I went home that day thinking, 'Well, what can we do as kids living on the island of Bali?' " Melati said in an interview.

Well, on Bali, the biggest problem wasn't hard to identify, since it was openly visible, right in front of the girls, on the beach next to their home. They would go swimming in the waters and find a plastic bag wrapped around their arms. They had to do something about this issue.

So what did they do? Start picking up the plastic bags

one at a time? That would've been more than enough for most of us, but not for these two.

They did some secondary research and discovered that 40 countries had banned or taxed plastic bags, discouraging their usage. The government needed to act- but it wasn't. Clearly, they needed some pushing. The sisters got some friends and started an online petition to ban plastic bags in Bali. Within 24 hours, 6,000 people had signed it. Simultaneously, they went out onto the beach and started beach-clean up campaigns. With haste, they began spreading awareness about their initiative, with school and community workshops around plastic pollution.

They shared their plans and projects on social media, and local media picked them up instantly. Soon, they were all over the news. They were not alone in wanting cleaner, more wildlife-friendly, local-friendly, and tourist-friendly beaches. Emulating Gandhi, they even went on hunger strikes in fury against the absence of a ban and political action.

The governor, Mr Pastika, had little choice but to respond.

The strike had gone on for only one day when the governor's office called them. The next day, they were picked up from school and escorted to the governor's office.

Pastika signed a Memorandum of Understanding with the sisters to work toward eliminating plastic on the island — and later pledged to rid Bali of plastic bags by 2018.

Come 2018, and there was no ban.

But they didn't lose heart. To meet with the senior most official on the island and get a concession from him was a big achievement, but they wanted more. Melati in particular, met regularly with politicians to discuss draft regulations and suggestions.

The sisters were tireless. They took part in dozens of speaking engagements internationally. Melati said she had spent 100 nights travelling in 2018-19, from everything from a TED Talk to a UN conference in New York and the IMF Forum at home in Bali.

The accolades, praise, and fame came streaming in.

In 2019, the governor of Bali announced a ban on single-use plastic. Melati and Isabel Wisjen, starting at the age of 13 and 11 and even then just 19 and 17, had pulled off a stunning feat, completely turning around the island's environmental fortunes, able to move the machinery of the government better than any NGO or environmental lobbying group.

But have they achieved what they set out to do? According to them, there's more they need to do.

Bye, Bye Plastic Bags has gone global, in 28 countries around the world.

Melati says she wants to continue demanding and creating change, and other young people to do the same.

"For us, everything is happening in our lifetime, right? So we have to be the ones to start working toward the future and the world that we want to be a part of."

YOUR GUIDE TO SAVING THE WORLD

From the sisters, we can take the lesson that even where we don't know what we will do to tackle immense issues far beyond us, just with a will to act and perseverance. There is also much we can do to have a positive impact on marine ecosystems, practically. Some of it is even simpler than beach clean-ups:

- Make dietary choices that help the seas- The fishing industry is extremely harmful to the seas, with overfishing and big nets like trawlers which often ravage ecosystems apart from just catching the needed fish. 95% of damage to seamount (seafloor) ecosystems, for example, is done by trawlers. Adopting a less fish and seafood-based diet could do these ecosystems a world of good. A quarter-vegetarian diet for one person saves 70 marine animals every year.

- Learn about beach clean-up-related projects in your neighbourhood and organisations that regularly conduct them- Public awareness is a key component of any community conservation initiative- without it, far fewer people would have joined the Versova beach clean-up. Gaining awareness online or by asking around is pivotal to participating in the most important movements in your community.

- Spread awareness regarding the necessity of beach clean-ups- Most people, as I did before I began working on this book, think that the sole role of beach clean-ups is removing litter thrown on beaches. However, that is far from the truth, as you know by now. It is the last line of defence against plastic entering and defacing our oceans and jeopardizing the marine life within. This will probably motivate many more to join such initiatives. Make sure to also inform your acquaintances about ways they can contribute and movements in your city they can support.

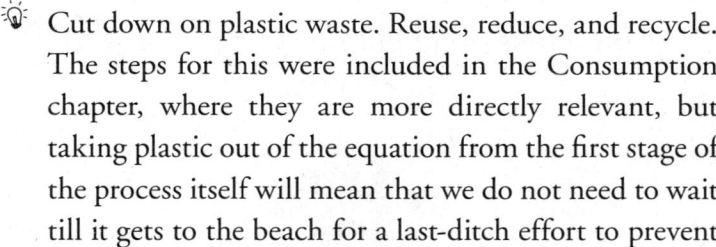 Cut down on plastic waste. Reuse, reduce, and recycle. The steps for this were included in the Consumption chapter, where they are more directly relevant, but taking plastic out of the equation from the first stage of the process itself will mean that we do not need to wait till it gets to the beach for a last-ditch effort to prevent it from reaching the sea.

David Attenborough

"The truth is the natural world is the most precious thing we have and we must defend it."

Chapter 16

THE LAND'S LEGENDS

I was born in Singapore. On May 7, 2008. In a land of asphalt and concrete and pavement and towering buildings. Safe, convenient, and comfortable. Also, artificial, insulated, and sterile.

I knew bird sounds to be irritating and blaring, like the screeches of sirens, from the loudspeakers nestled in the trees surrounded by shopping centres and hotels on Orchard Road.

Some days, I would be waiting for the school bus just outside my apartment, and I would see, on the ground during a rainy day, when it was coming down in torrents, the streets were soaked, and puddles were forming, ten-legged red millipedes wriggling their way through the flood, or tiny pink worms sinuously moving around at my feet. That was one of the rare instances when you could freely see wildlife in the midst of the urban sprawl.

Then, in April 2014, I came to Mumbai. I lived in Powai, and nature was suddenly far closer. Just behind my house, from the window, I could see hillsides, decorated with trees and bushes and grass in a glimpse of the wild beyond. In the distance, I could see the waters of Powai Lake. On the best of days, the lake would shine in the sun and melt my heart; on others, it would be covered in green beds of mysterious vegetation, floating upon it and masking the water below.

On the opposite banks of the lake were gently ambling slopes thickly blanketed in a forest.

One day, I asked my father what lay over there. "Animals?", I asked.

"Yes", he told me. "It is Sanjay Gandhi National Park."

A jungle in the middle of a city? Unbelievable!

In 2015, I went to the Park on a school trip and was awed by the sight of a magnificent white tiger- until it turned out to be a statue. My teacher told me it was an extinct species, and my heart broke.

We rode through the forest in a bus and gripped the window grills, and I placed my head on the ledge as I looked out into the eyes of spotted deer, herds roaming in the undergrowth that seemed to me like angelic beings from another world.

We congregated in the centre of the park to play some games, and a ranger spoke to us about the forest and its wildlife. "The park has 58 leopards", he was saying. "But it is very rare to see one".

I turned and saw, across the water of a wide river, a leopard.

It was wreathed in sunlight and with the still water reflected dimly by its body, which seemed to flicker and ripple just like the waves. It stood on its two front legs, its back ones lower, in a regal position, as its tail curled out on the floor, hazel eyes staring at me.

It was not deep gold but a faint shade of off-white with a brownish tinge. I made eye contact with it, as the fur on its skin stirred in the strong, chilly, breeze of the forest.

It was a fragile form, like a mirage. My soul said it was real but my mind couldn't wrap itself around and believe in the true existence, blood and sweat and skin, of such a delicate fantasy. But then, isn't all of nature like that these days?

I was speaking to my father a few months later. He said, "When I lived in Powai in 1996, all around us were forests. There were only maybe a handful of buildings."

"What happened to the forest?"

"People cut it down."

So that meant…the trees that lined every sidewalk, acting as a canopy for the streets with their wide boughs and sprawling crowns, were remnants from a paradise lost, a fantastical reality, that had vanished forever. I have walked amongst them deep in thought and spotted squirrels scurrying up and down the tree bark.

Over the years, I have regularly heard rumours, seen videos, and read breathless news stories, of wildlife in Powai. Leopards have prowled in the IIT campus; crocodiles have washed ashore on the roads when their homes have flooded in the rainy season; monkeys have climbed buildings and stolen food from the next-door apartment; people have returned home to find deer seated serenely on the floor.

They are vestiges of the past; the past we still remember, when they ruled the land and we were enterprising newcomers, and a past we will never know: the time before our species was born.

***

From very early on, the evidence was right before me. Animal extinction is often where we least expect it. Even the metropolis of Mumbai is haunted by the ghosts of a wild past.

Yet even they are faded and diminished after decades of development, tearing down the primaeval ecosystem of the land and replacing it with our structures of concrete and asphalt, supplanting worlds of rain and hunting and grazing and the growth of trees with the ascendancy of material progress.

Then, just like that, I forgot everything.

Between 2017 and 2020, I cannot remember devoting a single moment of thought and emotion to endangered animals and ecosystems.

I, against all my perceptions of my personality and nature, had become addicted to and locked in the classic 21st-century human rat race, pushing myself at academics in school and other things.

Even when I thought more broadly about the world and wrote my first books, I found joy and wonder not in tales of nature but in those of history- of great empires and wars and struggles to strive towards our ideals and glory. Of greedy humans seeking to manipulate the world to fit their own desires, putting down others of their kind.

When in 2020, I joined the Take the World Forward Fellowship and got an opportunity to pitch an idea for social change, that concern for the environment around us came back, and my desire to do something about it took a concrete form.

I do not know how that idea came back to me, how the dying embers from younger years kindled a new spark. But they did. I applied for a microgrant to research and write a book on animal extinction in urban areas from MIT SOLV[ED] and was awarded a grant.

I used this funding to research more about the issue, and what I discovered strengthened my conviction that this is a big issue.

46% of endangered animals live in cities. This should be obvious- after all, our development and urbanisation are what compromise the environment- habitat destruction, air pollution, and water pollution. But it is not.

I did a survey, and 99% of respondents said they associated endangered animals with the wilderness and national parks instead of cities. Ask yourself- before reading this chapter (or hell, even after reading it) would you be one of that 99%? Just a few years ago, I would have been part of that majority that is oblivious to the animal apocalypse happening around us.

Perhaps more concerningly- then again, perhaps just because people tended to view animal extinction as distant- 85% of respondents said the only way they thought they could contribute was by donating to NGOs.

So, I found out about a range of things we can all do in our daily lives to help out these endangered species. At times, it is strikingly simple actions that can make the biggest difference.

In April 2021, I published a book called *Back from the Brink: Join the War Against Animal Extinction*, which raised awareness of the issue of urban animal extinction, its magnitude, and how we can affect it, sharing real case studies of communities who had come together to make a difference and practical tips we could all employ. When I got many positive reviews on Amazon and Instagram, people telling me my book had inspired them and made them look at the issue through a different lens and encouragement and coverage in the national media, I felt a warm glow of happiness. At last, I had done something meaningful for something I cared about.

So, what were the actions I found out about? Surely I didn't fill a 200-page book with sentimental introspection and philosophising?

Let's travel to another fractured wilderness, across the ocean to get a better idea of the kind of steps I'm referring to.

***

TEEN HEROES WHO ARE SAVING THE WORLD

You are in Tanzania. Imagine you are an eight-year-old girl whose father and grandfather have fascinated you with stories of nature, from the Great Plains of your homeland to the Serengeti you are in right now.

The amber, golden-brown long grass of the savannah stretched into the distance like a sea of ochre. Three striped zebras stood there, munching the vegetation. The savannah meets a nebulous mass of blue and white at the horizon, like the thick strokes of an impressionist.

This is a work of art more beautiful than any you will find, perhaps because you can really feel the warmth of the sun on your skin and the wind blowing upon you softly like a storm of kisses. Perhaps just because the zebras are waving their bushy tails and munching, eyes reflecting daylight, shimmering with life. This is heaven.

Then heaven turns to hell.

You drive on the rocky, sandy path onward for a few minutes and spot a massive grey-red-white mass in the savannah. On it are heads grey as stone emerging from greyish-white ruffles of feathers, with beaks like sickles as they swing up and down with the precision of executioners, tearing out clumps from a colossal rock.

It very clearly is not a rock, though.

It has massive feet like pillars, with slightly curved feet and toes sticking out of them. It has immense, flopping ears and a nose snaking out and lying on the ground like a noose to hang criminals at the gallows.

An elephant.

Near its belly, there is an enormous hole, and through it, you can see the innards, of blood and marrow and bone and chunks of flesh.

One thing is conspicuously missing: the tusks.

This was the sight Annabel Caren Clark saw in 2012. Her grandfather, Jim Clark, had been a WWF member, and her father had taken her on numerous such trips to nature reserves due to his love for them, especially to the Great Plains of the Northern United States, where once roamed bison and burrowed prairie dogs in millions, a habitat today fractured by farms and cities and railroad tracks.

Annabel lives in Dallas, Texas.

There, the state insect is the Western Monarch Butterfly, given its name for its regal appearance and orange colour (two things associated with the 18th English King William, Prince of Orange). It is regarded nationally as one of the most beautiful animals, with its deep golden orange and slashes of black.

Since antiquity, it has been a symbol of sustenance and providence for the Native tribes.

The Hopi and Cherokee have special social dances recognising the butterfly for its beauty and its contribution to pollinating plant life. In doing so, these people displayed an extraordinary amount of ecological wisdom, one that's lacking in most of the modern world.

Even after invaders came from beyond the sea, the Monarch continued to find mainstream reverence in the continent of North America. It's the state insect of three

US states- Alabama, Texas, and Idaho.

But it seems that the respect and love of 300 million people wasn't enough to protect the butterfly. And why would it be, when behind a thin veil, all of the love and admiration is more feigned than real, at least for the governments and companies destroying the insect's habitat?

Industrialists razed fields of milkweed to the ground, and farmers poisoned them with fertilisers and pesticides. Milkweed is the very plant that Monarch larvae- babies- rely on for food.

In 1997, there were 1.2 million Western Monarchs. In 2019, there were 28,000.

Biologists, conservationists, and other experts said the end was nigh. 28,000 was lower than the butterfly's quasi-extinction threshold of 30,000- basically the point-of-no-return for the species.

But not everyone was this pessimistic. At least, Annabel wasn't.

She rallied her classmates in her school, and united them all with one common dream and plan- to plant Milkweed, and thus revive the dying populations of Monarch butterflies. They were all intrigued, perhaps by a love for the butterfly's appearance more than a desire to save the ecosystem.

Together, they amassed armies, armies of hundreds and hundreds of students, and teens who had very little expertise and know-how about what they were doing apart from a powerful drive and iron-hard will to restore some justice to the fortunes of the Western Monarch.

Annabel wasn't the only one. She was just one of many, one of many teens and adults working across the Western United States, from the Californian coasts to the Texan Plains, to instil some hope into the struggle to resurrect the Western Monarch Butterfly.

But with her spirit, she inspired hundreds of others to act, waking them from their slumber and showing them the dire nature of the butterfly's plight.

Within two years, 105,000 native plants, including 44,000 milkweeds, had been erected by volunteers.

In the 2021 count by the Xerces Society, 250,000 butterflies were found- a 12,400% increase from 2018. All thanks to courageous, driven, empowered teenagers like Annabel who proved to be more influential on the butterfly's comeback than the high-browed biologists behind the screens of their computers.

But even saving a few thousand Western Monarchs was not enough. Annabel and the community of environmentalists she had created wanted more.

She joined the Panda Ambassador WWF Program, becoming a "super-activist" who actually worked with the WWF to advocate for and even lead conservation efforts in the US and abroad.

At a smaller level, but one which continued to stimulate action and concern in her community, she founded the WWF Club, where teens and friends and classmates and anyone else could come to discuss conservation issues and understand them together, and take action as they had done with the Monarchs.

***

2007 was hot in Bavaria, Germany. The rays of the sun scorched the interiors of rocks, melted snow on mountain-tops, and set aflame the straws of reeds and the bark of wood on the forest floor, as wildfires raged.

Felix Finkbeiner was a 10-year-old student, and in a cool, air-conditioned classroom, his teacher asked him to do research on changes in the environment and their impact.

He learned two things: one, that his favourite animal, the polar bear, was becoming endangered. The second was a more positive finding- that planting trees is a solution. He read about Wangari Maathai, an African Nobel Peace Prize winner who planted 30 million trees in Kenya.

He presented these in class on Monday. "We must plant one million trees in every country in the world!", he proclaimed at the end.

If I said something like this in class, I'd get a few laughs and comments on my misplaced intensity and conviction. But Felix was serious, in the way only a 10-year-old can be.

In March 2007, his class planted a tree in front of the school. Other schools saw it and followed suit.

In one year, Germany had planted 50,000 trees. Felix made a website and organised planting competitions, attracting thousands of competitors across the country. He named his initiative Plant-for-the-Planet.

The German environment secretary noticed. The EU Parliament noticed. The UN noticed.

The UN had already started a project called the Billion Tree Campaign. But when the initiative of a 10-year-old overtook them in fame and results, they put Felix and his friends in charge of the Billion Tree Campaign too.

Over the next four years, Felix had led the planting of 12 billion trees. A couple more, and he'd done 15 billion.

Around 20 billion trees would absorb all the carbon dioxide India emits. Basically, Felix had had nearly as much impact as India would if it stopped emitting.

This unfolding of events seems crazy. We all talk about planting trees and afforestation, but most of us leave it on the pages of our school documents, the surfaces of posters, or the slides of a presentation. At school, especially in the IB system I study at, we talk about applied learning, but how many of us really apply what we learn about the environment?

But it seems insane for one teen's class presentation to lead to the planting of billions of them.

Now, Felix says he wants to plant a trillion; and you bet I believe him.

YOUR GUIDE TO SAVING THE WORLD

Fields with thousands of purple Milkweed flowers, forests with billions of trees…the thought of teens our age, or younger than us, making these possible is staggering.

To me, these two stories represent how we teenagers can sometimes make more change than those we usually depend on- the government or NGOs. Felix did better than the UN; Annabel did better than her government.

The ecosystem, after all, is a scientific, logical system of life that connects the whole globe. The steps that could heal it are thus simple and apply the way the system works.

- 💡 Planting native plants, and not planting exotic species: This is exactly what Annabel did, and just like in her case, native plants can be crucial lifelines for insects like bees. When we think of extinction, we usually think of big mammals- the lions or the elephants or zebras Annabel saw on her Kenyan trip, or the polar bear Felix loved. Intentionally choosing specific plants that help particular species is ideal. A quick Google search, for instance, revealed 19 plant species for bees. It can also be essential for the sake of the native plants themselves, which often suffer as cities grow and they are cut down in urbanisation or replaced with foreign species.

- 💡 Helping stray animals: giving one stray cat a home saves 8528 endangered animals in five years, including 2985 endangered ones. Let that sink in. Stray dogs and cats, abandoned and left to fend for themselves in the streets, are simply not evolved due to natural selection and adaptation to surviving alone in an urban environment. They have no natural prey or predator, and thus wreak havoc unchecked in urban ecosystems, sometimes travelling to suburbs or outskirts where there is more wildlife. Thus, stray cats have single-handedly caused the extinction of 63 species. Giving them a home by donating to stray animal shelters or even adopting one would make a big difference.

- Birdhouses: Birdhouses give birds safety, and shelter from the harsh urban environment where small birds like sparrows and mynahs struggle to survive as raptors like kites dominate. I made a birdhouse once, a simple one, done as a school project, and was elated to see, within a few days, a mynah was sitting beside it and inspecting it. Bird feeders can also be placed beside or inside birdhouses to make the house a true haven and home for the birds.

- Turning off the lights at night: Each home that keeps lights on at night after 11 pm kills a dozen birds every year. Birds, especially ones like parrots or mynahs or migratory ones not as used to urban life as species like pigeons or crows, get disoriented by this light as they mistake it for starlight, leading to collisions and severe injuries or deaths.

Benjamin Franklin

"Justice will not be served until those who are unaffected are as outraged as those who are."

Chapter 17

JUMPSTARTING JUSTICE

I'm lucky to live in a democracy, where people are free to speak their minds, elect their leaders, and news and social media are full of a plethora of points of view.

I thought this was how everyone lived since I was used to this kind of society. But as the years went on, I studied political systems at school and heard more tidings from the outside world. I learned about the dozens of dictatorships and authoritarian states that went against fundamental principles I had gotten used to, and often directly opposed democracy.

Recently, the media went wild over the Taliban invading Afghanistan and restoring a tyrannic, regressive government to the country. In Iran, a bank refused to serve a woman not wearing a *hijab*, and the nation erupted in protests.

Seeing that the world was far harsher and more fractured than I had believed, made me treasure what I had, and appreciate how fortunate I was to live in India.

When I turned to history books, they too told me that justice and peace do not come easily- they have to be earned, and created by battling the forces of avarice and bigotry that could undermine them. Often, common people must fight this war, from the Civil Rights Movement to anti-war movements. As recently as the 2010s, the Arab Spring's revolutions dethroned several tyrants in the Middle East, but often made political situations more precarious and violent, paving the way to years of civil war and discord. In Afghanistan, 2020, I was inspired by young women who stood tall in the face of the Taliban's oppression, fighting for their rights against a regime that saw them as not even deserving of education.

I realised that even though, outside a few regions, real wars and invasions were rare in today's world, true "peace" was elusive. On India's borders simmered decades-old tensions with Pakistan, and the minds of millions raged with abhorrence for the other. Israel and Palestine are launching rockets and artillery at each other, irreconcilable foes with millennia-old disputes beyond thought and memory.

The wars in the Middle East wrecked the homes of millions, who would flee to Europe in overloaded boats, or trudge through Greece and Albania. Waves drowned them, the snow froze them, guns shot them, and rocks scratched them. Even after that, most would be shut out forever, the door to the EU slammed in their faces, left alone, drifters with no food, water, shelter, or secure future.

Here were people with no home, forget big concepts of peace and justice and strong institutions. In the grand schemes of states, common people suffer.

Soon, it dawned on me: true peace stems from empathy; from compassion; from open-mindedness and a desire to accept other people for who they are. I took part in the Melton Foundation's Global Storytelling Festival, in which we had to write an ultra-short story, of less than 200 words, about finding common ground and bridging gaps between different cultures or peoples. I wrote a short story about an Indian and Pakistani boy becoming friends at an India-Pakistan cricket match, using their shared love for the sport, overcoming what their fathers had told them about "the enemy" and forces of geopolitics, religion, and history.

My story won first prize, but what felt more important was the realisation that all of us are more similar than we think, and understanding this can help us be kinder to each other.

Indeed, "peace" and "justice" sound like big words, more at home in a UN conference hall than in our everyday lives, but they start very close to us- in homes, schools, neighbourhoods, and communities. Bullying in schools and colleges is a microcosm of the injustice and repression we see around the world. Fighting bullying tackles conflict and injustice at a very fundamental level, a level at which millions feel their impacts every day.

There are teens who have applied this and made an

impact on peace and fairness in their countries, rising up against the forces of prejudice and strife that ran rampant in their world and their ancestors.

TEEN HEROES WHO ARE SAVING THE WORLD

In the Shark Tank India studio, a beautiful room of rich, brown floors ringed by lustrous, golden pillars, five judges sit, as they look ahead with a sense of intrigue.

Before them is a young girl in glasses, with curly hair, wearing black track pants and a pink shirt, smiling slightly nervously as she speaks about something she has made- an app, asking for funding at one of the best opportunities in the country for getting business investment and support.

But the journey here was a long and rocky one.

When she was 9, some of her closest friends bullied her. It broke her. She felt betrayed, powerless, and incompetent.

Once, at a school function, one of her friends was mocking a 6-year-old, putting him down and treating him like garbage. She didn't have the courage to speak up but felt numb as she watched.

On the school bus, she saw a 10-year-old boy sitting alone, with slumped shoulders, not meeting anyone's eyes. She asked him what was wrong, and he told her that some other kids on the bus had been bullying him. She encouraged him, not wanting him to face the same fate as her, to speak to his parents, which he did.

By now, she had seen way too much bullying around her for inaction. She would build an anti-bullying app.

First, she researched the issue, and learned a lot of

interesting things about what were some common threads when it came to bullying.

"It has to be done with an intention to hurt someone; It has to cause pain; It has to be repeated; There must be a power imbalance -- the person committing the act must be in a higher state of power or authority," she explained, in a Rediff interview.

"Indian kids are the most cyber-bullied (*in the world*). But most of the incidents go unreported. In fact, people don't even know where and how to report an incident of bullying."

The worst part was the lack of a reporting mechanism by hich the bullies would be dealt with- punishments for their misdeeds and prevention of recurring offences.

"Parents usually brush it off and don't take it seriously until it is too late", she said.

Her app would rectify this. She named it *Kavach*, meaning armour. Students could anonymously report incidents of bullying, "Sharing details of where the crime was committed", Anoushka said. The school authorities would receive alerts so they could investigate.

Her initiative was already gaining impetus and recognition before Shark Tank. In 2021, *Kavach* was voted one of the Top 21 for '21 Innovative Tech-Based Women-Led Startups by ITC and SheCapital.

In SharkTank, her idea was met with resounding approval, and she got Rs. 5 lakhs of funding.

She used that funding to start developing the app further, refining its User Interface and functioning. That was instrumental in transforming her dream into a living, breathing (or more like moving, vibrating) creation. By February 2022, 100 schools had used the app to benefit 2,000 students, and 1,000 schools had started the process of using it.

Going from not being able to protect herself from bullying to shielding tens of thousands, Anoushka's rise was meteoric and inspirational in how it illustrates our power to make society more peaceful and just.

***

2011. Waves writhe. Winds wreck. A storm strikes.
Yellow flashes in the sky. Voices cry. Hands flail.
There is a crashing sound, as the boat hits rocky ground. Men in orange and black scramble, and a family is found.
Thus came Josh Finkleman, 9, from Russia, to the shores of California.
Thus was determined his fate. Thus was made the fate of 5,000 others.
He settled, with his parents and grandparents, in San Diego. His father fell into poverty. In a strange new land with unknown people, systems, and customs, he struggled.
In the end, he scraped through, getting a job, and placing Josh into a decent school and lifestyle.
Six years later, in the back of his mind, Josh was not an American. He was a refugee, someone who had braved the seas and war to come to the promised land. A land where he had received precious little besides the most basic

of provisions: shelter, food, water, safety, and survival. That was more than enough if you led your life on the run as he had, but surely the world's richest, most powerful nation, home to billionaires and Silicon Valley and Hollywood, could do better?

He visited a refugee resettlement camp. Twenty children from all over the world gathered together, running around, and playing games, with not a care in the world. These very children- Josh empathised- once knew the blast of bombs and the burst of gunfire. Josh asked himself a very simple question. "What if they, like my father, fall into poverty?"

The voices of these children were neglected- cold, forlorn, lost souls left alone in their quest to settle in a new country.

They needed a voice- a voice equal to that of everyone else in society, what they deserved.

Thus was born the Equal Voices initiative.

"I am grateful that America let in my parents, grandparents, and all the refugees I have met, but we must work to keep it a land of opportunity if America is to remain beautiful."

Equal Voices would help those whose voices were forgotten.

And it did. Josh started small, taking classes with a few of the kids he met at resettlement agencies. Now, the initiative has blossomed and spread its bough to give a cool shade to thousands of young refugees, nurturing them and helping them prosper in a foreign land.

It teaches them skills like money management,

navigating public transit, CPR, and English, skills that Josh and his father had problems with when they were new to America.

Josh has done more than give these refugees equal voices. He has given them equitable opportunities, vital for their survival. He has spurred them on to succeed. He has made the United States of America more just.

YOUR GUIDE TO SAVING THE WORLD

Efforts to work towards this SDG can start small. Combating bullying is one way, not necessarily even making an app like Anoushka, but just doing what she did before that when she helped the boy by encouraging him to talk to his parents.

- Do not let yourself be bullied. Stand up to them by telling them that what they are doing is not right, and not being the helpless victim.

- Complain to parents or teachers. The higher authorities are there for a reason. Dealing with a bully yourself through confrontation beyond a point can be problematic and lead to escalation. Our parents and teachers are there to support us- we just need to know when to ask for help.

- Help friends or others you know who are being bullied. Bullying will be all around you, even if neither you nor your best friends are the victims. Support them, encourage them, and help them act such as complaining or speaking to the bullies.

Beyond that, learning more about the world- its political institutions, wars, rivalries, and coups- will help you understand this SDG better and the obstacles to its accomplishment. Keeping up-to-date with current affairs and reading the news is invaluable for this.

You could also take up activities like debating, including in formats like MUN, which give experience in analysing global issues from multiple perspectives. I have been debating with Speech Debate India for two years, and have explored a wide range of topics from NATO and the Russia-Ukraine conflict to military intervention in the Middle East and drug legalisation. Besides accumulating knowledge of these issues, I now can better appreciate the nuanced nature of our world and evaluate matters in a balanced way, forming more informed opinions.

In the end, the world around us is a big place, fraught with dangers and discord and enmities far deeper, older, and larger than us. But with a little bit of courage and initiative, we can make it a better place, just like Anoushka and Josh.

African Proverb

"If you want to go fast, go alone. If you want to go far, go together."

Chapter 18

PARTNERING TO CREATE A LEAGUE OF HEROES

Here, at the beginning of the final chapter, all the information in the previous one may feel overwhelming. There are so many things one can do, it seems, to save the world. But how does one even get started?

One of the biggest learnings I've had is that we're never alone in our quests to make the world a better place. We can always find allies and partners.

It starts with those closest to us- family, and friends.

In Tampa Bay, Demitrti and his waterway beads-removing organisation Green Gasparilla had his brother as a partner and later parents as support.

In Delhi, Armaan Singh and his school for slum kids had his mother, who gave up her job to help him run the place, managing a whole educational institution with dozens of kids.

In Santa Clara, Shubham Banerjee and his cheap Braille Printer Braigo had his father, the software engineer who guided him through all his failed prototypes and testing, and his mother who got him the kit that made it possible.

In Miami, Joshua Williams and the Joshua's Heart Foundation had his mother, grandmother, and six aunts, preparing and distributing every meal in the crucial early stages.

Then there are schools, classmates, and other such partnerships.

Taylor Thigpen, the Floridan boy who fought food wastage with share tables and decomposition in the school garden, worked closely with his school and eventually many others to implement his plan.

For my efforts to increase girl participation in Karate classes, I partnered with the Federation, discussing the issue and potential solutions.

For ThriftShift, we worked with our teachers and together as classmates, contributing to sustainable fashion and helping the underprivileged.

Then there are online communities, increasingly relevant in the digital age.

For *Back from the Brink*, I took advantage of lessons I learned at the Take the World Forward Fellowship by Learn with Leaders, learning from the stories and ideas of teens from around the world who were part of the programme, and benefitting from the microgrant funding and support from MIT SOLV [ED] for research.

Then there are organisations who welcome all help in

fulfilling their goals and tackling the problems they stand against.

Dola Akter Reba, in Bangladesh, became a member of World Vision, allowing her to save 600 girls from the clutches of child marriage.

Gideon Buddenhagen took his computers curriculum to Google, fuelling the tech giant's mission of spreading these skills to more people.

For *Underdogs*, I reached out to Save the Children, and their CEO, Mr Sudarshan Suchi's support and encouragement was invaluable.

For *Back from the Brink*, UNICEF helped with several ideas when I spoke to them, and their Director, Mr Rahul Bansal, has been an amazing mentor.

To combat the multitude of issues the SDGs look at, forging partnerships is essential as it brings greater unity and effectiveness to our quest to save the world.

At the end of this book, I think we should admire some of the amazing teens we've met, who were not already mentioned above, and how their stories are so similar yet so different.

Some of them started facing adversity and struggle personally and took others with them as they rose above it: Milan Kharkel in the Nepali village without electricity, Alfie Regan weighing 127 kgs, Anoushka Jolly being mercilessly bullied.

Many others, though, were not directly impacted but had the empathy and courage of conviction to act on issues they saw in the world around them- Shreya

Ramachandran, the inventor of grey water, seeing that the water crisis affected her just as much as California's weary farmers; José Quisocala, who became the world's youngest banker after seeing children selling food in the Lima's streets; Michelle Oyoo Abiero, who built a mental health campaign in Nigeria reaching hundreds based on her friend's plight; Anne Annabel Clark, who rallied her school around saving the Western Monarch, driven by her love of the butterfly and the wild.

SDG 11 was Sustainable Cities and Communities. Well, in many ways, we're all part of the same community- as the human race we share many issues and fates in common, from inequalities, poverty, and hunger to conflict, water loss, the climate crisis, and animal extinction.

And as teens, we are a community. Thus, it is important for us to share our ideas and brighten each other's lives and the lives of those we wish to help. Post on Instagram with #teensguidetosavingtheworld, tagging me with @aadityasenguptadhar. Share your ideas, share your concerns, and share stories of teens who inspire you.

We are a community of young people thrown into the most chaotic century ever without choice. We did not choose when we would be born, or the problems that the world we are born in is afflicted by.

But we can choose what kind of world we inherit as adults. We can choose whether we remain apathetic to the problems around us, or step up like the many teens whose stories I've shared in this book.

We can choose to be bystanders. Or we can choose to be heroes.

Individually, we are just kids. Together, we can save this world.

BIBLIOGRAPHY

POVERTY PULVERIZERS

Paliath, Shreehari. "A Year after Exodus, No Reliable Data or Policy on Migrant Workers." *Www.indiaspend.com*, 24 Mar. 2021, www.indiaspend.com/governance/migrant-workers-no-reliable-data-or-policy-737499.

World Bank. "COVID-19 Leaves a Legacy of Rising Poverty and Widening Inequality." *Blogs.worldbank.org*, 2021, blogs.worldbank.org/developmenttalk/covid-19-leaves-legacy-rising-poverty-and-widening-inequality
"Young Activist Sets up Bank to Tackle Poverty and Environmental Damage." *OHCHR*, www.ohchr.org/en/stories/2022/01/young-activist-sets-bank-tackle-poverty-and-environmental-damage

HUNGER GAMES HEROES

"Teen Creates Programs and Raises Funds to Address Classmates' Hunger." *Www.usdairy.com*, 18 Aug. 2018, www.usdairy.com/news-articles/teen-volunteers-food-insecurity-classmates. Accessed 15 Feb. 2023.

Drake, Diana. "Teen-Led Businesses Tackle the Problem of Food Waste." *Wharton Global Youth Program*, 6 Dec. 2018, globalyouth.wharton.upenn.edu/articles/environment/teen-businesses-tackle-food-waste/. Accessed 15 Feb. 2023.

"Teen Fights Global Hunger and Poverty with 'Heart.'" *Maria Shriver*, 14 Jan. 2018, mariashriver.com/teen-fights-global-hunger-and-poverty-with-heart/
"10 Ways to Get Kids to Waste Less Food." *Ivaluefood.com*, 2014, ivaluefood.com/resources/cooking-eating/get-kids-to-waste-less-food/.
Smith, Shea. "Teaching Kids about Food Waste." *Threeoclockproject*, 12 Nov. 2019, www.threeoclockproject.org/post/teaching-kids-about-food-waste.

WELLBEING WARRIORS

Bour, Hayley Milon. "Two Teens Develop App to Improve Mental Health." *LoudounNow.com*, 5 Nov. 2021, www.loudounnow.com/news/education/two-teens-develop-app-to-improve-mental-health/article_ca9d24bf-bc36-5828-8221-5577aa068ba7.html.

"MICHELLE OYOO ABIERO." *We Are Family Foundation*, www.wearefamilyfoundation.org/gtl-2020/michelle-oyoo-abiero.

Baggett, Lauren. "75% of Teens Aren't Getting Recommended Daily Exercise." *UGA Today*, 25 Aug. 2022, news.uga.edu/75-of-teens-arent-getting-recommended-daily-exercise/

"Teen Helping Others Get Fit after Shedding Seven Stone Himself." *Daily Echo*, 17 Aug. 2022, www.dailyecho.co.uk/news/20661558.southampton-teen-helping-others-get-fit-shedding-seven-stone/.

Flockett, Anna. "Screen Time Has Increase by 76% during the COVID-19 Pandemic." *Startups Magazine*, 2021, startupsmagazine.co.uk/article-screen-time-has-increase-76-during-covid-19-pandemic.

EDUCATION ELECTRIFIERS

Taylor & Francis Group. "Underprivileged Teenagers More Likely to Give up Their University Ambitions." *ScienceDaily*, 22 June 2017, www.sciencedaily.com/releases/2017/06/170622110446.htm.

Foundation, Smile. "Promoting STEM Education amongst Girl Children & STEM Jobs for Women." *Smile Foundation*, 21 Mar. 2021, www.smilefoundationindia.org/blog/promoting-stem-education-amongst-girl-children-stem-jobs-for-women/.

for Child, Child. "CFC in Conversation with Shivani Shrotri." *Www.youtube.com*, 2021, www.youtube.com/watch?v=-6MvcNwuY2g. Accessed 15 Feb. 2023.

Chakraborty, Ajanta. "Kolkata Teen Sets up NGO to Educate Street-Kids." *The Times of India*, 13 Sept. 2019, timesofindia.indiatimes.com/city/kolkata/kolkata-teen-sets-up-ngo-to-educate-street-kids/articleshow/71111871.cms.

Team, TBI. "5 Ways You Can Start Educating Underprivileged Children Right Now." *The Better India*, 6 May 2015, www.thebetterindia.com/23037/5-ways-in-which-you-can-start-educating-underprivileged-children-right-now/.

GENDER EQUALITY GALVANIZERS

Tu, Jessie. "5 Teenage Activists Fighting for a Better World." *Women's Agenda*, 12 Oct. 2020, womensagenda.com.au/latest/5-teenage-activists-fighting-for-a-better-world/.

Livio, Sara. "How Youth Can Take Action to Ensure Gender Equality." *GLOBAL YOUNG VOICES*, www.globalyoungvoices.com/fast-news-blog/2018/4/3/how-youth-can-take-action-to-ensure-gender-equality.

WATER WARRIORS

"6 Teens Solving World Water Challenges for a Cleaner Planet." *Global Citizen*, 25 Aug. 2016, www.globalcitizen.org/en/content/6-teenagers-solving-world-water-challenges/.

Deaton, Jeremy. "Teen Scientist Finds a Low-Tech Way to Recycle Water." *Discover Magazine*, 28 Jan. 2021, www.discovermagazine.com/environment/teen-scientist-finds-a-low-tech-way-to-recycle-water.

Kamin, Debra. "Saving Water, with Kids Leading the Way." *Www.timesofisrael.com*, 11 July 2013, www.timesofisrael.com/saving-water-with-kids-leading-the-way/.

"Worldwide Water Shortage by 2040." *ScienceDaily*, Aarhus University, 2014, www.sciencedaily.com/releases/2014/07/140729093112.htm

"2.1 Billion People Lack Safe Drinking Water at Home, More than Twice as Many Lack Safe Sanitation." *Www.who.int*, 12 July 2017, www.who.int/news/item/12-07-2017-2-1-billion-people-lack-safe-drinking-water-at-home-more-than-twice-as-many-lack-safe-sanitation.

GROWTH GENERATORS

"Meet the 13-Year-Old Who Invented a Low-Cost Braille Printer." *Smithsonian Magazine*, www.smithsonianmag.com/innovation/meet-13-year-old-who-invented-low-cost-braille-printer-180956659/.

Deffree, Suzanne. "Shubham Banerjee: The Brains and Heart behind Braigo Labs." *EDN*, 30 Jan. 2015, www.edn.com/shubham-banerjee-the-brains-and-heart-behind-braigo-labs/. Accessed 6 Mar. 2023.

ENERGY EXEMPLARS

Rathi, Akshat. "The Teenager Who Could Change the Way the World Fights Climate Change." *Quartz*, 8 Dec. 2017, qz.com/1132303/the-teenager-inventor-who-could-change-the-way-the-world-fights-climate-change.

"Nepal Teenager Invents £23 Solar Panel." *Www. climatechangechallenge.org*, www.climatechangechallenge. org/News/Green-Inventions.

INNOVATION ICONS

Ruiz-Grossman, Sarah. "Teen Girls Create Apps to Tackle Gender Violence, Clean Water Access in India Slum." *HuffPost*, 10 May 2016, www.huffpost.com/entry/dharavi-girls-india-apps_n_5730f3b0e4b016f37896b547. Accessed 16 Feb. 2023.

Drake, Diana. "'Sit with Us' Creator Natalie Hampton's Crusade to Help Bullied Teens Feel Included." *Wharton Global Youth Program*, 27 Sept. 2016,

globalyouth.wharton.upenn.edu/articles/podcasts/sit-us-creator-natalie-hamptons-crusade-help-bullied-teens-feel-included/. Accessed 17 Feb. 2023.

Grasyte, Ruta. "Teen Who Used to Be Bullied Creates 'Sit with Us' App That Helps Students Find Lunch Buddies." *Bored Panda*, 2017, www.boredpanda.com/sit-with-us-school-lunch-app-natalie-hampton/. Accessed 3 Mar. 2023.

Factfile: Dharavi. Biddenam School, www.biddenham. beds.sch.uk/wp-content/uploads/2020/05/Enl-May-7Geo4.pdf.

EQUALITY ENTHUSIASTS

Hwang, Janice. "This Biracial Jewish Teen Is Helping Bring Computer Coding to Young Students of Color." *Jewish Telegraphic Agency*, 1 Sept. 2022, www.jta.org/2022/09/01/united-states/this-biracial-jewish-teen-is-helping-bring-computer-coding-to-young-students-of-color.

CNN, Tami Luhby and Christopher Hickey. "US Black-White Inequality in 4 Charts." *CNN*, 1 June 2021, edition.cnn.com/2021/06/01/politics/black-white-racial-wealth-gap/index.html.

Inequality.org. "Global Inequality - Inequality.org." *Inequality.org*, 2019, inequality.org/facts/global-inequality/.

Neate, Rupert. "Richest 1% Own Half the World's Wealth, Study Finds." *The Guardian*, The Guardian, 27 Nov. 2017, www.theguardian.com/inequality/2017/nov/14/worlds-richest-wealth-credit-suisse

SUSTAINABILITY SUPERSTARS

Bhowal, Sayantika. "Mumbai's Ayaan Shankta Wins Global Accreditation for His Eco-Conscious Project." *Digpu.com*, 9 Sept. 2021, digpu.com/achievers/ayaan-shankta-wins.
Staff, Washington Post. "12 Kids Who Are Changing Their Communities and Our World." *Washington Post*, 11 Apr. 2020, www.washingtonpost.com/kidspost/2020/04/11/12-kids-

who-are-changing-their-communities-our-world/.

AP. "Nigerian Teens Create Fashion from Trash to Fight Pollution." *The Times of India*, 22 Nov. 2022, timesofindia. indiatimes.com/home/environment/nigerian-teens-create-fashion-from-trash-to-fight-pollution/ articleshow/95682305.cms.

---. "Fashion from Trash... Welcome to Nigeria's 'Trashion' Show." *Euronews*, 22 Nov. 2022, www.euronews.com/ culture/2022/11/22/fashion-from-trash-welcome-to-nigerias-trashion-show. Accessed 16 Feb. 2023.

Davies, Richard. "The Importance of Waste Segregation | Axil-IS Blog." *Axil Integrated Services*, 9 Sept. 2021, axil-is. com/blogs-articles/waste-segregation/
"Kolkata Teen Sets up NGO to Educate Street-Kids." *The Times of India*, 13 Sept. 2019, timesofindia.indiatimes. com/city/kolkata/kolkata-teen-sets-up-ngo-to-educate-street-kids/articleshow/71111871.cms

"36% Indian Kids Lacked Internet Access during Covid Lockdown: Report." *The Times of India*, 12 Nov. 2021, timesofindia.indiatimes.com/education/news/36-indian-kids-lacked-internet-access-during-covid-lockdown-report/articleshow/87671663.cms.

"5 Ways You Can Start Educating Underprivileged Children Right Now." *The Better India*, 6 May 2015, www.

thebetterindia.com/23037/5-ways-in-which-you-can-start-educating-underprivileged-children-right-now/.

ROLE MODELS OF RESPONSIBILITY

AP. "Nigerian Teens Create Fashion from Trash to Fight Pollution." *The Times of India*, 22 Nov. 2022, timesofindia.indiatimes.com/home/environment/nigerian-teens-create-fashion-from-trash-to-fight-pollution/articleshow/95682305.cms. Accessed 16 Feb. 2023.

Warming Solutions, Global. "The Fashion Industry Waste Is Drastically Contributing to Climate Change." *CALPIRG*, 9 Mar. 2021, pirg.org/california/articles/the-fashion-industry-waste-is-drastically-contributing-to-climate-change/#

---. "Fashion from Trash... Welcome to Nigeria's 'Trashion' Show." *Euronews*, 22 Nov. 2022, www.euronews.com/culture/2022/11/22/fashion-from-trash-welcome-to-nigerias-trashion-show.

CLIMATE CHANGEMAKERS

Ghosh, Niharika. "Riddhima Pandey - the 11 Year Old at the Forefront of Climate Activism in India." *Homegrown*, homegrown.co.in/homegrown-explore/lifestyle/riddhima-pandey-the-11-year-old-at-the-forefront-of-climate-activism-in-india. Accessed 16 Feb. 2023.
Maharashtra's Controversial Aarey Forest Project, Why Is It Resurfacing Time and Again? 1 July 2022, www.

outlookindia.com/national/maharashtra-s-controversial-aarey-forest-project-why-is-it-resurfacing-time-and-again--news-205977

Kamenetz, Anya. "NPR Choice Page." *Npr.org*, 2020, www.npr.org/2020/01/19/797298179/you-need-to-act-now-meet-4-girls-working-to-save-the-warming-world. Accessed 19 Jan. 2020.

Pinter, Jacob. *Young Activists Can Sue Government over Climate Change, Supreme Court Says.* 11 Mar. 2018

Susmita Baral. "6 Ways to Help Fight Climate Change." *Teen Vogue*, Teen Vogue, 23 Oct. 2017, www.teenvogue.com/story/6-ways-to-help-fight-climate-change

UNDERWATER UPLIFTERS
Sullivan, Michael. "NPR Choice Page." *Npr.org*, 26 Jan. 2019, www.npr.org/sections/goatsandsoda/2019/01/26/688168838/how-teenage-sisters-pushed-bali-to-say-bye-bye-to-plastic-bags

"Afroz Shah and UN Environment Celebrate 100-Week Anniversary of World's Largest Beach Cleanup...with Another Cleanup." *UN Environment*, UN, 4 Oct. 2017, www.unep.org/news-and-stories/press-release/afroz-shah-and-un-environment-celebrate-100-week-anniversary-worlds

Harish. "How Many Animals Does a Vegetarian Save?" *Countinganimals.com*, 6 Feb. 2012, countinganimals.com/how-many-animals-does-a-vegetarian-save/.

THE LAND'S LEGENDS
"Cullum and Annabel Clark on the Power of Family." *World Wildlife Fund*, www.worldwildlife.org/magazine/issues/winter-2016/articles/cullum-and-annabel-clark-on-the-power-of-family. Accessed 17 Feb. 2023.

"Plant-For-The-Planet – Trillion Trees for Climate Justice." *Plant-For-The-Planet*, www.plant-for-the-planet.org/

Parker, Laura. "Teenager Is on Track to Plant a Trillion Trees." *Science*, 7 Mar. 2017, www.nationalgeographic.com/science/article/felix-finkbeiner-plant-for-the-planet-one-trillion-trees

JUMPSTARTING JUSTICE
Nair, Divya. "'Indian Kids Are the Most Cyber-Bullied.'" *Rediff*, 24 Feb. 2022, www.rediff.com/getahead/report/anoushka-jolly-why-this-teen-built-an-anti-bullying-app/20220224.htm.

Kaplan, Arielle. "These Jewish Teens Are Helping Refugees Thrive in Their Hometowns." *Hey Alma*, 24 Jan. 2020, www.heyalma.com/these-jewish-teens-are-helping-refugees-thrive-in-their-hometowns/.

Saxena, Akanksha. "13-Year-Old Girl Creates 'Kavach' App to Combat Bullying in Schools, Secures Rs 50 Lakh Funding." *Thelogicalindian.com*, 14 Feb. 2022, thelogicalindian.com/uplifting/anti-bullying-app-kavach-33939. Accessed 17 Feb. 2023.

Kaplan, Arielle. "These Jewish Teens Are Helping Refugees Thrive in Their Hometowns." *Hey Alma*, 24 Jan. 2020, www.heyalma.com/these-jewish-teens-are-helping-refugees-thrive-in-their-hometowns/. Accessed 16 Feb. 2023.

ABOUT THE AUTHOR

Aaditya Sengupta Dhar is a budding teenage author with four published books to his name. He loves using his imagination to create fantastic new worlds. He published his first fantasy novel, *Secret Tails*, at the age of ten and his 2023 fantasy novel, *Legend of the Broken* Blade, was a bestseller.

Aaditya also aspires to use his writing to make a difference in causes he's passionate about. His 2020 eBook, *Underdogs*, raised awareness of the importance of helping underprivileged children unleash their potential, with all sales proceeds donated to Save The Children India. His 2021 book, *Back from the Brink*, highlighted the largely unknown issue of animal extinction in urban areas and how we can all make a difference through simple, everyday tips.

Outside of school and writing, Aaditya is a passionate Cricket fan and student of Karate, in which he holds a Black Belt.

Aaditya is fourteen years old and lives in Mumbai.